THE STORY OF T
WIL
WEST

er.
DEALERS
tLouis LagerBeer
DENTIST
BANK.
STEBBINS, POST & CO.
JOB PRINTING
LS TIMES
RED BIRD.
MARKET

THE STORY OF THE WILD WEST

Robin May

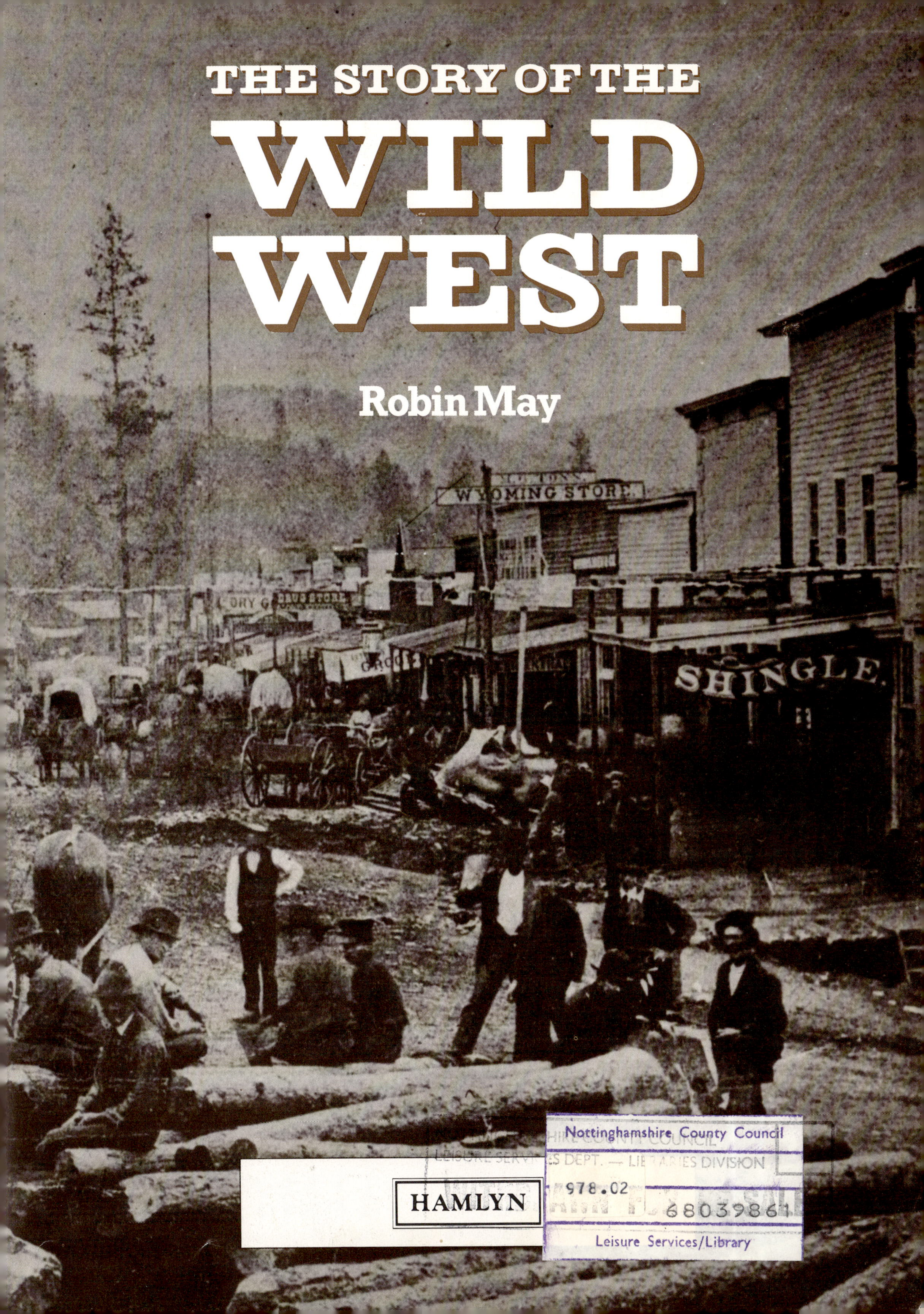

HAMLYN

To Jeff Burton and Colin Rickards of the English Westerners' Society

endpapers
Road workers display their grisly find during grading work on 'Boot Hill' outside Hays City, Kansas. The anonymous inscription is possibly the work of the photographer.

title spread
Deadwood in 1876, the archetypal wild boom town, made suddenly rich in the Black Hills gold rush.

Published by
Hamlyn Publishing
Bridge House, London Road, Twickenham, Middlesex

Second impression 1986

ISBN 0 600 50301 1

Filmset in England by Tradespools Limited,
Frome, Somerset
Printed in Portugal by Resopal

Contents

Chapter 1

Why the West was Wild

The Wild West, a compound of violence, bravery and squalor, boredom and high adventure, endurance and sudden death, is usually taken to mean the period between the end of the Civil War in 1865 and the turn of the century. This book is mainly concerned with the Gunfighter's West, and homesteaders, railroad workers, rivermen, Indians and others will only occasionally appear on the scene.

There were a number of 'Wests' before the most famous one, some of them even wilder, and in this brief prelude we will be examining several of them. For the Wild West did not suddenly come into being. Its roots were deep in American history, though today all too many of the facts about it are shrouded in myths. The Code of the West, for instance, is one of the great myths perpetuated by Hollywood, with formal shoot-outs at a distance in dusty streets. The real code, such as it was, went as follows: shoot an unarmed man and it counts as murder, but if he was armed, even if he was facing the wrong way or was sound asleep, then you will probably get away with a plea of self-defence at your trial. The dead man's friends, however, may lynch or shoot you.

opposite
Charles R. Jennison, leader of Jennison's Jayhawkers, one of many outfits that made Kansas and Missouri bleed before and during the Civil War.

above
A heavily armed band of Kansas Free Staters celebrating the fact that they had rescued John Doy (seated) from jail in July, 1859.

right
This typical Western posse was photographed after capturing a gang that had tried to rob a bank at Medicine Lodge, Kansas, in 1884. Three of the gang were later lynched.

above
'The Mountain Man' by Frederic Remington. Mountain Men, who trapped beaver when their fur was high fashion early in the nineteenth century, were probably the toughest men who ever roamed the West.

right
James 'Jim' Bowie, famed as a duellist and for the knife that bore his name – and for his death at the Alamo.

below
A Bowie knife *c.* 1850, with a blade $9\frac{1}{4}$ inches (23.5 cm) long.

opposite
Early days in Deadwood.

But this is not a debunking book. The gunfighters, within or without the law – and many changed sides more than once – are presented neither as heroic supermen nor as dastardly villains, nor, as too often happens nowadays, as homicidal maniacs. Rather are they shown as human beings in violent times, exceptional only in their readiness to kill if necessary and having the right technique to do so. And the violence of the times is indicated by a statistic accepted by many experts. Between 1866 and 1900 some 20,000 died of 'lead poisoning'.

The first Anglo-American West, unless the Englishmen who landed at Jamestown in 1607 and Plymouth Rock in 1620 are included, happened in the mid-1770s when the American Revolution was raging. Men, women and children crossed the Appalachians into Indian territory – Kentucky's 'dark and bloody' ground and beyond.

These intrepid, land-hungry, restless Frontier people knew violence well, as their ancestors had. And the Revolutionary war on the Frontier was a vicious civil war between rebels and loyalists, with Indians usually on the King's side on the principle that they had more chance to hold their lands if the King won. They chose wrongly. After the war the Border remained a dangerous place for travellers. The terrors of Indian wars in the forest were less, for soon the tribes were being driven westwards, but white killers lurked along the Ohio, the Natchez Trace, and the Wilderness Road, killers like the terrible Harpes, whose butcheries were so vicious that even their brothers in infamy completely disowned them.

In the South violence varied from gentlemanly duels with pistols to no-holds-barred fights with knives, guns and fists, biting and eye gougings included.

The Southwest, into which Spaniards had marched as early as 1540 searching for mythical cities of gold, knew all the violence of Indian, especially Apache, wars in the centuries that followed. Meanwhile, the Frontier people had advanced westwards, spurred on by wanderlust, leaving behind those who wanted permanent roots. The Louisiana Purchase of 1803, the best land deal in history, saw the United States obtain the entire region from the Mississippi to the Rockies from France. After Lewis and Clark had made their famous expedition of 1804–6 to the Pacific and back, the way was wide open for the Mountain Men, the toughest men who ever roamed the West, to seek fashionable beaver fur, blaze new trails, fight Indians, marry them and become virtually white Indians. Jedediah Smith, Jim Bridger and Kit Carson are the best remembered. And while they lived life to the full, a short life in many cases, Southerners had gone to settle in Texas. The immortal Alamo episode (1836) is yet another aspect of violence as the Texans broke away from Mexico and won their independence.

The 1840s saw the great crossings to Oregon, another chapter in the story of the Frontier people, but it was the finding of gold in California in 1848 that brought thousands round the Horn, across Panama and along the most direct route across the Plains. And now there was violence on a vast scale, violence and anarchy. The mainly peaceful, backward Indians of California were almost wiped out; the Chinese were victims of racial hatred; law and order were virtually non-existent. In booming San Francisco order was maintained by vigilantes, who acted grimly but responsibly, then disbanded. In many other parts of the West vigilantes were to be mere lynch mobs.

A typical lynching was vividly described by Edward Buffum, a journalist turned miner. Five men were caught robbing a gambler and were given thirty-nine lashes each, but three of them were then accused of murder and an attempted armed robbery that had occurred some months before. Two hundred 'jurors' sentenced them to death. The trio could not plead in English, two being French and one Chilean.

above
Miners at work in Deadwood in 1876. Especially in their early days, most mining camps had virtually no law and order except lynch law.

left
It was a Wild West custom to have one's photograph taken. Here are three New Mexican cattle rustlers following the fashion.

below
Helena, Montana, started life as Last Chance Gulch: prospectors struck gold just when they were about to give up.

above
John Brown was given this Navy Colt, but the donor so objected to his proposed raid on Harper's Ferry that he left it behind.

below
John Brown's Colt ·36 Navy revolver, 1851 Model, now at the Kansas State Historical Society, Topeka.

opposite
John Brown was a murderous fanatic, but his 'soul goes marching on' forever because of his abortive attempt to stir up a slave revolt and his subsequent execution.

Buffum spoke up for them and was nearly hanged himself. As for the men, 'Vainly they called for an interpreter, for their cries were drowned by the yells of the now infuriated mob . . . the wagon was drawn from under them, and they were launched into eternity.'

Mining areas were never less than lively and violence was never far below the surface, though few suffered as much as Montana in 1864, when a master criminal, Henry Plummer, was conducting a brilliant reign of terror. Despite a violent past elsewhere, no-one realised what he was doing. One look at him and it was clear he was a man to be trusted, and this notable con-man excelled himself by getting elected as Sheriff of Bannack, which made it that much simpler to run his army of highwaymen, known in the locality as 'road agents'. Plummer built a string of lodging houses near the mines, all of them staffed by his men. Each stagecoach that was worth robbing was marked, while his gang, who called themselves 'The Innocents', wore special knots in their neckties for identification. Finally, this Napoleon of crime was suspected, and vigilantes ended his notable reign in their by now traditional manner – in this case utterly justified.

Worse even than the goldfields at their most turbulent was the situation in Kansas and Missouri in the 1850s. Murderous pro-slavery gangs battled with equally murderous anti-slavery gangs. Young Wild Bill Hickok wrote home to his mother that Kansas was no place for women and children yet. Kansas 'Free-soilers' and Missouri's pro-slavery Border Ruffians got in some excellent training for ruthless guerilla campaigns in the Civil War. The Border Ruffians were on the whole more murderous than their rivals, invading Kansas, looting, burning and killing anyone who dared try and defend his family. The opposition had its own answer in the fiery, fanatical John Brown, who in these years before his soul went marching on staged an atrocity appalling even by 'Bleeding Kansas' standards.

right
The notorious Southern guerilla leader, William Clarke Quantrill.

opposite, left
'Bloody Bill' Anderson's guerilla gang in the Civil War included the James boys and the Youngers.

below
Bear River City, Wyoming, a typical 'Hell on Wheels' end-of-track town that sprang up during the building of the Union Pacific Railroad. Some, like Cheyenne, survived to become cities.

below
John Heath was lynched at Tombstone, Arizona, in 1884, after planning a robbery in which he did not take part. The citizens objected to his twenty-year sentence, stormed the jail and put a telegraph pole to drastic use.

above
Vigilante justice, Texas style, in 1881. The culprit seems doomed to be 'jerked to Jesus'.

right
The most famous battle of the Indian Wars – Custer's Last Stand – took place at the Little Big Horn in Montana in 1876. This is the aftermath: the bones of some of Custer's men.

below
Three men charged with murder in Kansas ended their lives in an unusual setting.

above
'A Fight in the Street' by Frederic Remington.

One May night in 1856 the town of Lawrence had been looted by Border Ruffians, but no-one had been killed. In revenge (and some say to settle a personal score) Brown and his murderous offspring descended on log cabins at Pottawatomie Creek, along with two other henchmen. They were armed with guns and razor-sharp broadswords and they dragged five innocent farmers from their homes and butchered them. Apologists did their best later to absolve the murderous martyr from guilt, but in 1878 one of the gang came forward to clinch the facts many already knew.

The Civil War on the Border became an extension of these bloody conflicts. As early as September 1861 the first major atrocity occurred when ex-Free-stater, General James Lane, pursued General Sterling Price into Missouri on a retaliatory raid. As he went, he began punishing those who had allegedly helped Price and soon his

right
Dead soldiers in Hays City, 1873. One David Roberts had shot them both.

above
Black soldiers guarding a Concord coach.

opposite, above
The population of Guthrie, Oklahoma, sprang from 0 to 10,000 one day in 1889 when Indian land was opened to whites. Pictured is a family holding down a lot.

opposite, below
Geronimo (on horseback, left) and Naiche (also mounted), the son of Cochise, pictured in 1886, the year that the Apache Wars finally ended.

men were looting and murdering. Nine men at Osceola were 'court-marshalled' and shot and most of the town was destroyed. The worst guerilla leader of all, William Clarke Quantrill, was spurred by this atrocity to side with the South. He gathered a choice band around him, notably 'Bloody Bill' Anderson, Frank James, the Youngers, and other young killers. On 21 August 1863 they took revenge for the killings at Osceola, attacking Lawrence, Kansas, with more than 400 men. Lane was there and escaped unharmed, but the town was destroyed and 150 perished.

Frank James fought with Anderson when 'Bloody Bill' became commander of his own band, and the seventeen-year-old Jesse James joined him, getting some excellent training for his later exploits.

When peace came in April 1865, the stage was set for the saga of the Wild West to begin. The pattern of violence has been traced, and it only remains to add the bitterness of defeat in the South as a further cause of yet more violence to come. And there was the extra ingredient of Southern cowboys meeting Northern marshals in cowtowns. That lay in the future. Now, hundreds of thousands of men were demobilised and the vast majority returned home to lead decent lives. We are more concerned with those who did not.

Holding Down A Lot In Guthrie.
26

below
The road to high adventure, or boredom and discomfort, or sudden death.

bottom
In the heart of the Canyon de Chelly, Arizona, an unlucky traveller contemplates his shattered wagon.

Chapter 2

The Robber Bands

The James Gang

Nowhere in Missouri had there been so much hatred and bitterness between Union and Confederate supporters as in the Northwestern counties of the state, and one of those was Clay County, where Frank James had been born in 1844 and his brother Jesse in 1847. Their later notoriety magnified and distorted their exploits in the bloody guerilla warfare that was described in the last chapter, and we can never be sure just how much their outlawry acted as a natural outlet for their own lethally anti-social qualities and how much it owed to the savagery of the raids and massacres that wracked the Kansas-Missouri border during the Civil War.

In 1865, just at the close of the war, Jesse James was so badly wounded that he was lucky to survive. By the time he had recovered, most of the surviving guerillas had been paroled by the victorious Northern forces, but some simply did not want to live in peace, and some of their neighbours who had fought on the other side would not let them live in peace anyway.

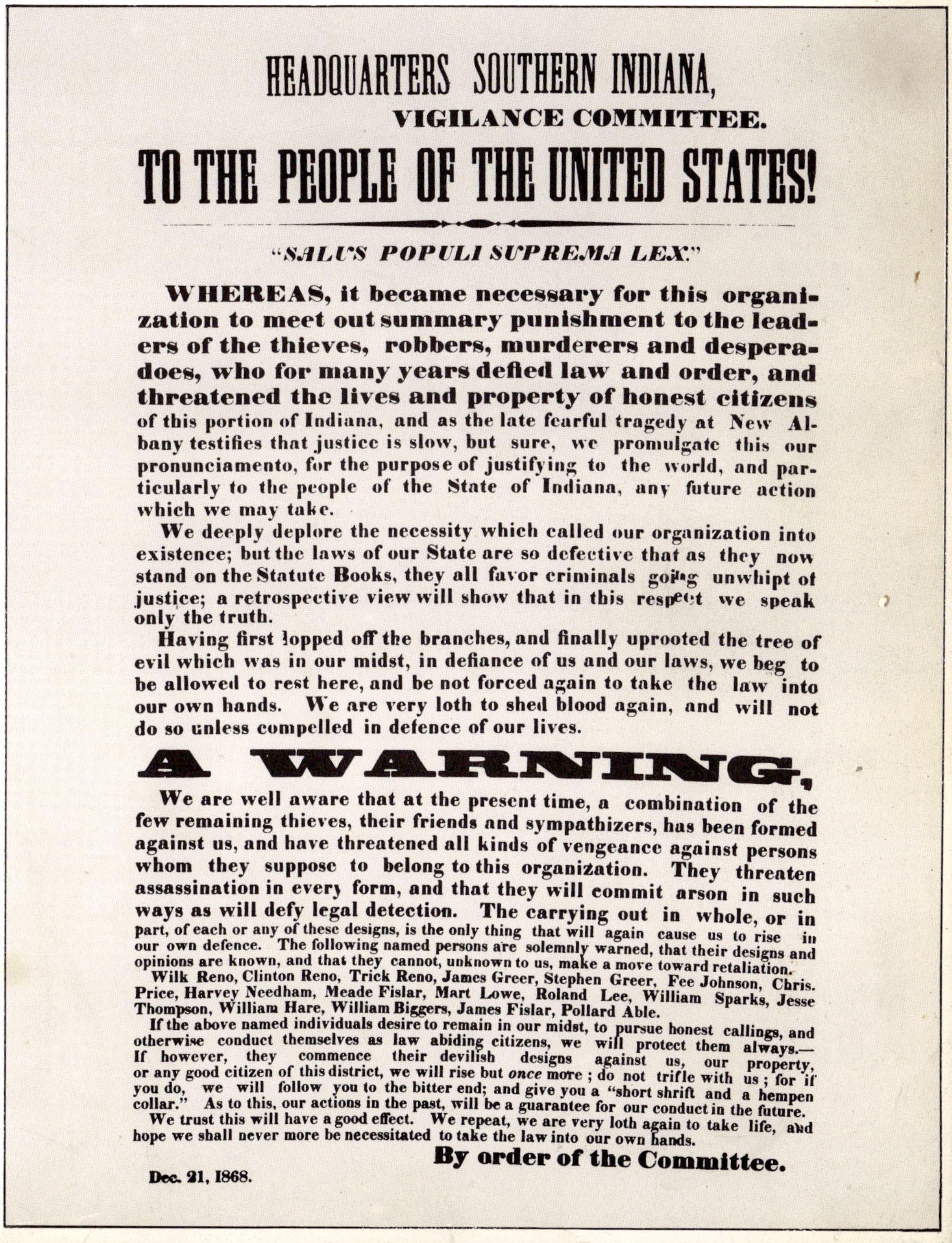

HEADQUARTERS SOUTHERN INDIANA,

VIGILANCE COMMITTEE.

TO THE PEOPLE OF THE UNITED STATES!

"SALUS POPULI SUPREMA LEX."

WHEREAS, it became necessary for this organization to meet out summary punishment to the leaders of the thieves, robbers, murderers and desperadoes, who for many years defied law and order, and threatened the lives and property of honest citizens of this portion of Indiana, and as the late fearful tragedy at New Albany testifies that justice is slow, but sure, we promulgate this our pronunciamento, for the purpose of justifying to the world, and particularly to the people of the State of Indiana, any future action which we may take.

We deeply deplore the necessity which called our organization into existence; but the laws of our State are so defective that as they now stand on the Statute Books, they all favor criminals going unwhipt of justice; a retrospective view will show that in this respect we speak only the truth.

Having first lopped off the branches, and finally uprooted the tree of evil which was in our midst, in defiance of us and our laws, we beg to be allowed to rest here, and be not forced again to take the law into our own hands. We are very loth to shed blood again, and will not do so unless compelled in defence of our lives.

A WARNING.

We are well aware that at the present time, a combination of the few remaining thieves, their friends and sympathizers, has been formed against us, and have threatened all kinds of vengeance against persons whom they suppose to belong to this organization. They threaten assassination in every form, and that they will commit arson in such ways as will defy legal detection. The carrying out in whole, or in part, of each or any of these designs, is the only thing that will again cause us to rise in our own defence. The following named persons are solemnly warned, that their designs and opinions are known, and that they cannot, unknown to us, make a move toward retaliation.

Wilk Reno, Clinton Reno, Trick Reno, James Greer, Stephen Greer, Fee Johnson, Chris. Price, Harvey Needham, Meade Fislar, Mart Lowe, Roland Lee, William Sparks, Jesse Thompson, William Hare, William Biggers, James Fislar, Pollard Able.

If the above named individuals desire to remain in our midst, to pursue honest callings, and otherwise conduct themselves as law abiding citizens, we will protect them always.—If however, they commence their devilish designs against us, our property, or any good citizen of this district, we will rise but *once* more; do not trifle with us; for if you do, we will follow you to the bitter end; and give you a "short shrift and a hempen collar." As to this, our actions in the past, will be a guarantee for our conduct in the future.

We trust this will have a good effect. We repeat, we are very loth again to take life, and hope we shall never more be necessitated to take the law into our own hands.

By order of the Committee.

Dec. 21, 1868.

The Renos were train and bank robbers. Three of them had just been lynched.

The new pattern of Border violence erupted on Tuesday afternoon, 13 February 1866, when between ten to thirteen men descended on the small town of Liberty, Missouri, while most of the populace were enjoying a trial in the Justice Court. The band, less three men who acted as guards, headed for the Clay County Savings Association Bank and robbed it of $57,000 in bonds and currency and from $5,000 to $15,000 in gold coin. As they left town a youth named George 'Jolly' Wymore was quite needlessly slain while he stood on the opposite side of the street.

Brutal murder was an old story on the Border, but armed bank robbery was shockingly new. Indeed, apart from a daring raid on several St. Alban's, Vermont, banks by a Confederate officer in 1864, no-one had tried this particular form of adding to one's income – and the earlier endeavour had been patriotic.

In later years it was assumed that the James brothers took part in the raid and – by many – that Jesse was the leader. But though even writers who should have known better stated flatly that the brothers were there, all that can be said is that Frank probably was and that Jesse may have been. The raid occurred near their home and the leader may have been Arch Clement, a killer whose exploits in the war had been notorious. He was Frank's best friend and was one of the only guerilla leaders not to be granted a parole, and Jesse hero-worshipped him.

A chilling feature of the Liberty raid was the marksmanship of the gang, the wretched Wymore receiving four bullets from one rider, any of which, it was later stated, would have been fatal.

The next raid was on a bank at nearby Lexington where the robbers expected to draw $100,000 but had to settle for a mere $2,000 because the vault could not be opened. Arch Clement, the probable leader here, as before, rode to his death in an ambuscade on his next visit to Lexington, but it made no difference: the robberies went on, the James boys being in some of them but not yet as ringleaders.

Before continuing the saga of bank robberies leading up to the birth of the James gang as such, it is worth asking how the robbers managed to retain so much public sympathy. In the war it had been different: they had been regarded by half the population of the state as patriots, even if some of them did take scalps. But now?

The answer must be that many Southern farmers, their farms ravaged by troops and guerillas of both sides, desperately needed money to restore their farms to prosperity and they found that the local bankers, whatever their politics, were tight wads who charged exorbitant rates of interest. Naturally, this coloured the farmers' attitudes to the current activities of the erstwhile guerillas.

A third hold-up, at Savannah, brought no booty, and a fourth, in which between a dozen or a score of riders stormed Richmond, killing three men besides robbing the bank, led to the lynching of several actual or alleged members of the gang. In contrast, the fifth raid – at Independence, in northwest Missouri – was accomplished with a notable lack of commotion by the robbers, who evidently knew that the First National Bank would still be open at 5 pm that particular day. (Banks even then generally shut their doors at 3 pm.) It should be noted that the robbers never neglected to steal bonds which could be – and were – quite easily and safely encashed.

Jesse James was among the seven or eight who planned the bank robbery at Russellville, Kentucky, in March 1868, but he was not

opposite
Jesse James, alleged by some to have been a Robin Hood. The evidence for such a claim is non-existent.

right
The corner of the yard where Jesse James was buried near Kearney, Missouri, though his body was later removed to a cemetery. The old lady is his mother.

below
In his old age Frank James put his lurid past to sound commercial use.

among the five who actually showed up and departed with some $14,000. Cole Younger, now 24, was, as a new recruit, one of the five, and it was he who held a gun at the head of the bank's elderly president, Nimrod Young. The spunky old man made a break for it and reached the street with no more than a crease in his scalp, and soon hastily armed citizens were on the streets. The gang escaped, but one of them, the over-confident George Shepherd, shouted to a bystander: 'You needn't be particular about seeing my face so well you'd remember it again.'

He was rewarded for his foolhardiness by a three-year stretch in jail, for the citizens of Russellville, and particularly the bankers, were eager for vengeance. A large posse had no success, so a detective from Louisville, one D. G. Bligh, was hired to trace the culprits, a novel hazard for the Missouri robbers. The outcome was a raid on Shepherd's home.

Jesse and Frank were back in action on 7 December 1869, at Gallatin, Missouri, Jesse in the meantime having been baptised in the presence of his formidable mother, Zerelda Samuel, who had been widowed before the war, then married again. The Kearney Baptist Church had been the scene of Jesse's apparent conversion to righteousness, but the prospect of what was to be had from the Daviess County Savings Bank at Gallatin was too much for him.

The brothers worked on their own, and the result was 700 bloodstained dollars, for the cashier was shot dead for no apparent reason. Of course, a reason has been advanced – that the unfortunate cashier looked like a damned Yankee officer whose men had succeeded in killing Bloody Bill Anderson back in the good old guerilla days. Naturally, patriotism banished all thoughts of baptism. . . .

The brothers had a running fight to get out of town, with Jesse forced to exit clutching on to Frank, as his own mare had bolted. The horse was later identified and the boys were mentioned in the local press and branded as outlaws. A three-thousand dollar reward was offered and a saddened – and still free – Jesse wrote to the *Kansas City Times* claiming not only that he had not robbed the bank at Gallatin but that since the war he had 'lived as a peaceable citizen, and obeyed the laws of the United States to the best of my knowledge'.

He wrote to the right organ, for the Editor was firmly Confederate

below
An artist's impression of the Northfield raid in 1876 which saw the end of the James–Younger gang.

bottom
A view of Main Street, Northfield, *c.* 1870, six years before the James–Younger gang made their disastrous raid.

and was soon perpetrating the myth of two heroic veterans being persecuted by Authority for their wartime activities.

In June 1871, Frank, Jesse and some three or four of their close neighbours in Clay County plotted the robbery of the bank at Corydon, Iowa. The four who actually performed the deed got back to Missouri with a little more than $5,000, a sizeable sum in those days, but far short of the $40,000 legend has credited to them. They had, however, made a memorable impression on Corydon, for when they had grabbed the loot, they rode to a church where most of the populace was gathered outside, enjoying or otherwise the efforts of a politician. Jesse interrupted the proceedings, announcing: 'We've just been down to the bank and taken every dollar in the till.' Then he and his companions lifted their hats, let out some exultant war whoops, and vanished at a gallop.

This, and not, as has so often been claimed, the robbery at Liberty, was the true start of the

'James gang' as such. The James–Younger gang went into action in Kentucky on 29 April 1872, when the two Jameses and Cole, Jim and John Younger, swooped down on the bank at Columbia, murdered the cashier, and made off with about $1,500, a modest reward for a foul day's work.

The next ten years are a chronicle thick with robbery and mayhem, an outline description of which would look rather like the Book of Numbers, brightly painted, as Jeff Burton has aptly written. But before picking out the highlights, a little light relief is in order. On 26 September 1872, the Jameses visited the annual Kansas City Fair, leaving with the contents of the cashier's safe. Later Wild Bill Hickok was credited with frustrating their activities, but the great man was not at the fair until the next day, when he cheekily forbade the band playing 'Dixie' to the fury of every unreconstructed Confederate present.

Meanwhile, a reporter of similar sentiments wrote a stirring account of the dashing James boys which so delighted them that they paid him a visit, bearing a gold watch.

The startled journalist refused the gift, thinking it was stolen property. 'Heck no,' said a hurt Jesse. 'This'un we bought with our own money.' When the reporter still refused to accept their gift, a hurt Jesse looked seriously at him and said: 'Well, then perhaps you can name some man around here you want killed?'

The Jameses and the Youngers robbed banks and trains (the first of these in 1873), but they also robbed stagecoaches and stores as well, and even these specialities were not all. Take the year 1874:

Thursday, Jan. 8 – Two stagecoaches near Arcadia, Louisiana.
Thursday, Jan. 15 – Stagecoach near Malvern, Arkansas.
Friday, Jan. 30 – Steamboat at Point Jefferson, Louisiana.
Saturday, Jan. 31 – Train on Iron Mountain Railway at Gad's Hill, Missouri.
Wednesday, Feb. 11 – Store at Bentonville, Arkansas.
Wednesday, March 11 – A Pinkerton detective murdered in Jackson County, Missouri.
Tuesday, March 17 – Two more detectives and John Younger killed in St. Clair Co., Missouri.
Tuesday, April 7 – Stagecoach between Austin and San Antonio, Texas.
Sunday, August 30 – Two omnibuses in area of Lexington, Missouri.
Monday, Dec. 7 – Bank at Corinth, Mississippi.
Tuesday, Dec. 8 – Train on Kansas Pacific Railway at Muncie, Kansas.

This is a truly remarkable catalogue of crime. Some of the relative dates and locations serve as proof that the 'James–Younger gang' was often composed of two or even more distinct bands, for there is not the least doubt that all of these coups were the handiwork of the Jameses, their allies the Youngers, or various of their other cronies.

It was in 1874, too, that both James boys found time to get married, first Jesse to his cousin Zerelda Mimms (though he had been briefly married to someone else before this), then Frank to Annie Ralston, a farmer's daughter. All round, it was quite a year.

By now public sympathy had turned away from the James boys, as it was bound to after such exploits. It swung back dramatically. The well-known Allan Pinkerton, whose story belongs to Chapter Three, had been called in to help lead the fight against the gang, and, as the list for 1874 shows, had lost some men in the process. It was extremely hard to get an undercover agent into the heartland of the gang in Clay County, but at last agent Jack Ladd, working as a farm hand, was located just across the road from Mrs Samuel's home. In January he spotted the Jameses and managed to get a message out which brought a posse of Pinkerton and local detectives into the area. They surrounded the robbers' nest and tossed a metal object into it which they later claimed was a flare to let them see their target. James supporters never wavered from the belief that it was a grenade.

COLE YOUNGER
After prison release
- 1901 -

One of the household shovelled it into the fireplace and it exploded, killing Mrs Samuel's nine-year-old son by her second marriage, Archie, a fragment of metal casing hitting him. And poor Archie's mother had her right forearm almost torn off, so much so that it was later amputated.

She at once went to work to inform the public, appalled at the event, that her beloved boys had not even been at home on the fatal night. From now on far too many Missourians and others saw the Jameses as martyrs, and the by now deeply unpopular Pinkertons broke cover and embarked on a campaign of harassment that got them exactly nowhere. Indirectly, however, it led to the downfall of the gang, for, deciding to venture far more deeply into the North than in the past, the Jameses planned a raid on the bank at Northfield, Minnesota, in which everything that could go wrong did go wrong.

above
After his release from prison, Cole Younger joined with Frank James on a lecture tour about the evils of crime.

opposite, left
Bob Younger died in prison in 1889 after surviving the Northfield raid.

opposite, right
Twenty-five years after the Northfield raid, Jim Younger was released from prison.

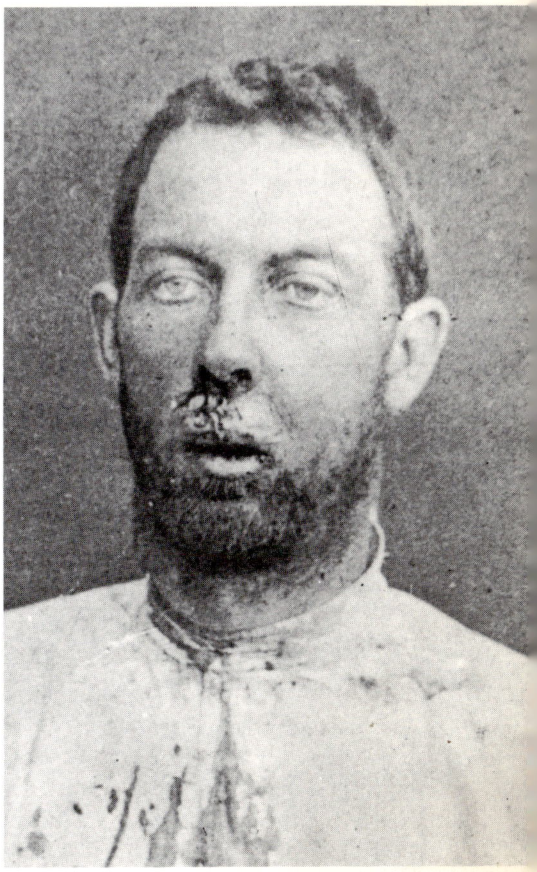

They planned their northern trip carefully enough, visiting a number of towns as land speculators and cattle traders and enjoying local amenities like a brothel at St. Paul, and a gambling house, and finally selecting Northfield and its First National Bank as their target. They carried out what should have been a reasonable reconnaissance on 6 September, then returned on the morning of the 7th, bound for catastrophe and near annihilation.

While five of the gang whooped it up and loosed off shots that suitably scared bystanders, Jesse, Bob Younger and Charlie Pitts ran into the bank and ordered: 'Throw up your hands!' The brave cashier, Joseph Heywood, reached the vault just after Pitts and vainly tried to slam the door on him. Then Jesse arrived and ordered him to open the safe. Heywood told him it had a time lock and could not be opened.

'That's a damned lie,' shouted the furious Jesse and felled him with his revolver.

Meanwhile, one of the two clerks, A. E. Bunker, had managed to break out through the bank's back door while Bob Younger was looking at the till, and, though Charlie Pitts winged him, he made his escape.

There were valiant men in Northfield who refused to be cowed by the gang, and, though they were short of firearms, they made the most of those they found in the town's two hardware stores – which had been cased the day before by the gang. In a few minutes four men died – two of the raiders, Clell Miller and Bill Chadwell, a Swede who blundered into the firing line, and the cashier Heywood. He had only been stunned by the blow from Jesse's revolver, but the callous 'Robin Hood' from Clay County is said to have seen him lying on the floor as he was leaving the bank and shot him through the temple. However, it is now thought that Frank killed him.

The Minnesotans had not finished with the invaders yet. It took twenty or so furious minutes for the remnants of the gang to break out, and not before a young medical student, Henry Wheeler, had hit Bob Younger in the thigh, hardware merchant A. E. Manning had first killed Chadwell, then hit Cole Younger in the shoulder, Jim Younger had been hit in the face, and Frank James in the leg.

However, six out of eight of the gang were alive, though with all

below
The house in which Bob Ford killed Jesse James in 1882.

opposite, above
Jesse James's killer, Bob Ford, was branded 'a dirty little coward' but his record was less deplorable than that of the man he killed.

opposite, below
Jesse James in death.

Minnesota in an uproar when news of the Northfield battle broke, the survivors were soon in trouble again. Scores of citizens were soon out after them.

The gang split up when, four days after the raid, posses seemed to be closing in from every direction, and Jesse, unharmed at Northfield, was hit by a bullet that went through Frank's knee and ended in his brother's thigh. However, the pair finally made it back to Missouri.

No-one else did. The three Youngers, along with Pitts, were cornered near Madelia, in a thicket where Charlie Pitts met his end. Finally, only Bob Younger was on his feet, though wounded, and he called out: 'The boys are all shot to pieces. For God's sake don't kill me!' They didn't, and with notable restraint the Minnesotans did not lynch the brothers, but allowed justice – in the shape of life imprisonment – to take its course. Bob Younger died in prison in 1889, Cole and Jim being released in 1901. Jim was soon to kill himself, but Cole teamed up with Frank James lecturing on the evils of crime.

Jesse kept away from outlawry for three years after the Northfield fiasco, his brother for four and a

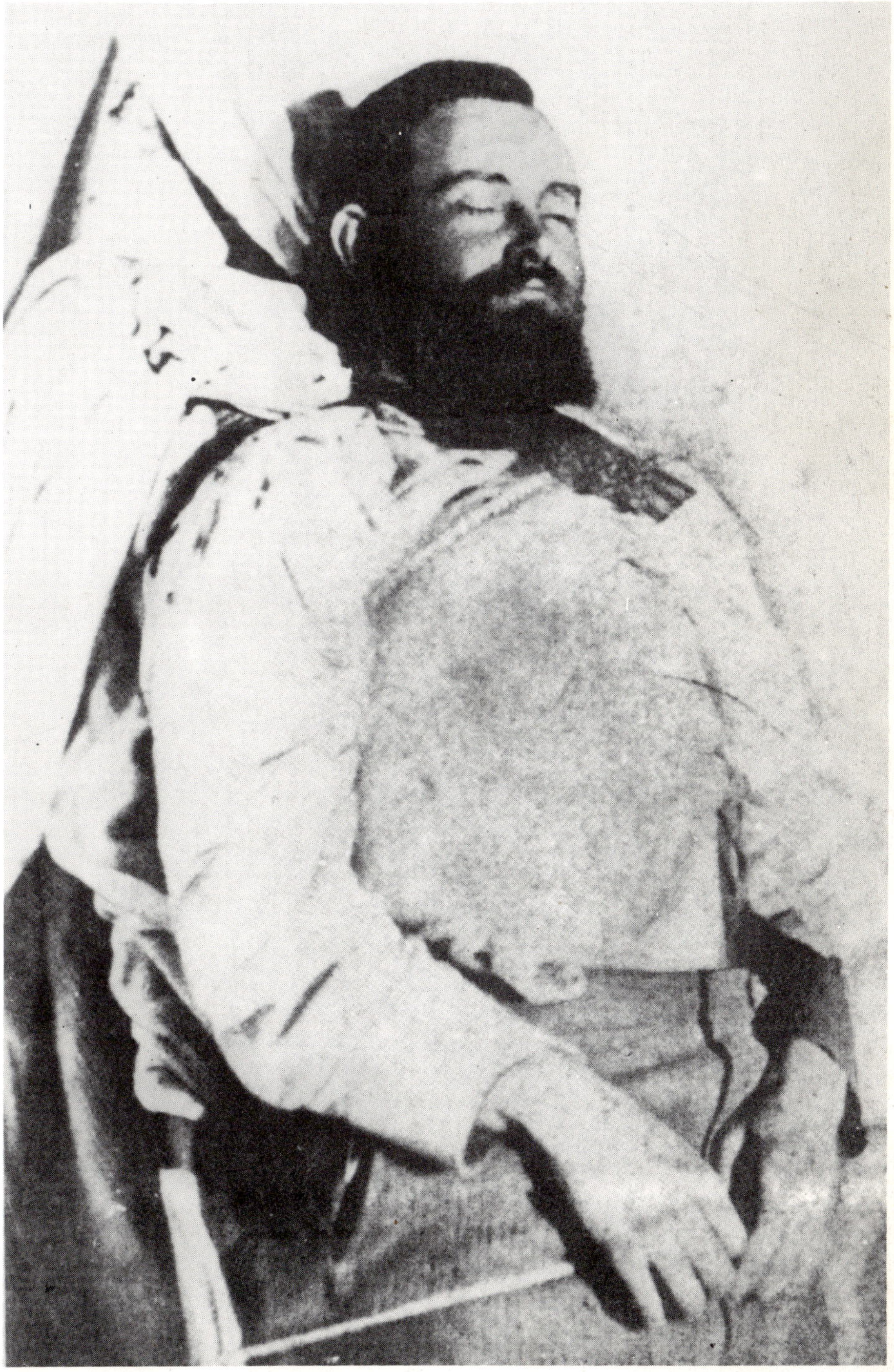

half. With so many men after them, they tended to avoid their native haunts more often than not, and when they visited Missouri they preferred to stay in Kansas City. Years later Frank pointed out to a reporter that the 'best hiding place in the world for a man with money is some big city. Most people look alike there.' It helped, of course, that the firm of Pinkerton had not yet developed its system of mug shots to a fine art, hence the story of how Jesse, along with his doctor who treated him for his gunshot wound after Northfield, dined at the same table in a Fulton, Missouri, hotel with a number of Pinkerton men. Jesse, murderer and thief, certainly had panache.

The brothers and their wives lived in Tennessee for a time, but in 1879 Jesse returned to Missouri, where he raised a gang who collected $6,000 from the Chicago & Alton Railroad train at Glendale, Missouri. Though Jesse returned safely to his home in Tennessee, one of the gang was caught and named his leader. It was the beginning of the end, and the pot really boiled over when a train robbery at Winston, Missouri, produced two more murders. The date was 15 July 1881, and Governor Thomas Crittenden swiftly persuaded the Missouri railroads to underwrite rewards of $10,000 for the arrest and conviction of the two Jameses.

In a show of force, Jesse gathered a band of twelve or more, half of them untried but willing local louts, and robbed another train near Kansas City, Missouri. This, on 7 September 1881, was his last throw, panache included, for he gave the engineer two dollars with which to drink his health the next morning. As for Frank, by now he was beginning to tire of outlawry.

Behind the scenes there was so much dealing and double-dealing between officials and bandits, between officials and friends of bandits, and between one set of officials and another, that the exact truth is not easy to find. Yet all that matters is that Governor Crittenden – quite illegally – decided to have Jesse James killed by one of his own gang. Jesse was now living in St. Joseph, Missouri, under the name he had used publicly since his Tennessee days, J. D. Howard. He and his wife and two children, Jesse and Zee, settled down in a house on a hill in November 1881. On Monday morning, 3 April 1882, Bob Ford honoured his contract with a single skull-shattering bullet.

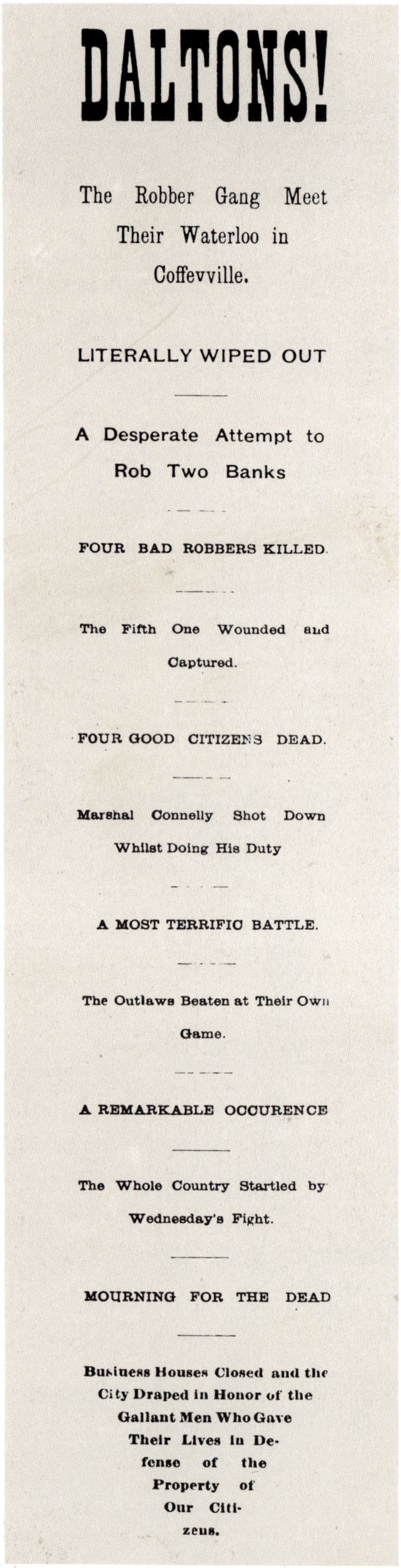

DALTONS!

The Robber Gang Meet Their Waterloo in Coffevville.

LITERALLY WIPED OUT

A Desperate Attempt to Rob Two Banks

FOUR BAD ROBBERS KILLED.

The Fifth One Wounded and Captured.

FOUR GOOD CITIZENS DEAD.

Marshal Connelly Shot Down Whilst Doing His Duty

A MOST TERRIFIC BATTLE.

The Outlaws Beaten at Their Own Game.

A REMARKABLE OCCURENCE

The Whole Country Startled by Wednesday's Fight.

MOURNING FOR THE DEAD

Business Houses Closed and the City Draped in Honor of the Gallant Men Who Gave Their Lives in Defense of the Property of Our Citizens.

right
A Kansas paper's summary of the events of the Coffeyville raid in October 1892.

opposite
The Condon Bank at Coffeyville, one of the two banks the Daltons aimed to rob.

Jesse was unarmed at the time and, according to what Ford told Crittenden, standing on a chair with his back to him, and dusting a picture on the wall. Jesse heard the hammer of Ford's gun click as he cocked it with his hand, and began to turn as Ford pulled the trigger. The bullet hit him just behind the ear and he 'fell like a log, dead'.

Bob Ford, who was tried and sentenced to death, then rapidly pardoned by Crittenden, was himself murdered ten years later by a man named Kelley. Ford has been reviled as a traitor and characterised in a famous song as the 'dirty little coward who shot Mr Howard'. As the pro-James section of the Press had lamented Jesse's death with banner headlines suitable for the fall of a hero, this was hardly surprising. Yet Ford, if hardly an admirable citizen, was certainly no coward, and he was no more of a traitor than Jesse, who, time and again, quarrelled with, lied against, and informed upon those who had sheltered him and those who had robbed with him. Many tears have been shed for Jesse James, all of them misguided. In his last months he was surrounded by traitors, but they had all been bred by the violence and instability of his own nature.

As for brother Frank, devotee of Shakespeare and Francis Bacon, six months after his brother's death he handed his revolver – unloaded – to Crittenden in person. There were a good many influential Missourians who, for all sorts of reasons, wanted Frank to get clear of the charges against him. And wonderful as it may seem now, he was convicted of nothing. He might – he should –

have been convicted in Minnesota, but Minnesota was not allowed anywhere near him. He lived quietly, dully even, shooting off guns only as a starter at county fairs and the races, and he admitted people to the 'Home of the James' for fifty cents – before dying at the age of seventy-one, thirty-two years after the State of Missouri had tried him for the murder of a passenger during one of his train robberies – tried him but let the Southern hero go free.

The Daltons

Of all the gangs that sprang into being in the wake of the James boys and the Youngers, none came to a more spectacular end than the Daltons. They were kinsmen of the Youngers and part of a large family who lived at Coffeyville in southern Kansas. Lewis and Adeline Dalton had fifteen children, the four to become notorious being Grat, Emmett, Bob and Bill.

Another brother, Frank, acted as a deputy US marshal under 'Hanging Judge' Isaac Parker for a time, but he was shot and killed in 1887 when attempting to arrest three whiskey peddlars in Indian Territory, the notorious area which –

BOB
Copyrighted by Tackett
-No.

opposite
Bob and Grat Dalton, dead or dying.

above
The end of the Dalton gang. Left to right: Bill Powers, Bob Dalton, Grat Dalton, Dick Broadwell. Emmett Dalton survived and Bill Dalton missed the raid, being killed in 1894.

along with Parker – will feature in the next chapter. Grat and Bob both became lawmen, Emmett worked on a ranch and Bill got married and appeared to have settled down.

This respectability did not last. Grat and Bob were implicated in disposing of stolen livestock, Bob also killing a man over a woman, while Emmett began horse stealing. Along with Bill, who is generally thought to have planned many of the gang's robberies, the by now outlaw brothers became among the many scourges of Indian Territory. They worked with others until deciding to form a gang to rob their own home town. Robbing trains was not exciting enough.

Crazily, they decided to rob two banks at once, taking along two others, Tim Evans and Dick Broadwell. They rode into Coffeyville on 5 October 1892 minus brother Bill.

Certain features of the raid would seem almost comic if the results had not been so tragic: the street between the banks was under repair unbeknown to the Daltons, who were forced to leave their horses half a block away; the absurd moustaches and false beards; the lack of proper planning . . . A passer-by recognised Emmett and Bob while they were helping themselves to some $20,000 at the First National Bank and ran into the square calling: 'The Daltons! The Daltons!' At once, the town was aroused, men arming themselves with their own guns or ones rapidly borrowed from the store.

Across the street at the Condon Bank, Grat, Emmett, Evans and Broadwell were also in trouble, for the brave teller informed his visitors that the bank's vault had a time lock which could not be opened. The delay this caused enabled the infuriated citizens to prepare for action and, as the gang tried to make a break for their horses, a gun battle erupted. When the smoke cleared it was found that four citizens had died defending their town and that all the Daltons except Emmett were dead or dying, and so were their accomplices.

Emmett was given life imprisonment at the Lansing penitentiary but was lucky enough to be pardoned fourteen years later, after which he headed for California. He became an adviser for Westerns in Hollywood and actually wrote books and features on law and order, and he died of natural causes in 1937.

One young associate of the Daltons, Bill Doolin, had the luck not to be included in the Coffeyville fiasco. He was to be far more successful than any of them, but his story belongs to the next chapter. As for Butch Cassidy and the Wild Bunch, the last of the great robber bands, they will be featured in Chapter Seven which, as it is entitled 'End of an Era', is most emphatically where they belong. As for the Daltons, perhaps a local paper's report on their final effort should end this chapter – 'One of our banking institutions was visited yesterday by the firm of Dalton Brothers for the purpose of closing large accounts. When the transaction was completed they had been paid in full with interest compounded.'

Chapter 3

Rough Justice

James Butler 'Wild Bill' Hickok, the 'Prince of Pistoleers'.

Marshals and Sheriffs

The sensible lawman knew the facts of Frontier life. Said Wild Bill Hickok in 1871: 'If you have to shoot a man, shoot him in the guts near the navel. You may not make a fatal shot, but he will get a shock that will paralyse his brain and arm so much that the fight is all over.'

In the previous chapters the first, rather haphazard attempts to bring law to a violent West were noted. Here the emphasis is on the taming of the cowtowns and the war against the outlaws in Indian Territory, as well as the growth of law enforcement agencies.

Before gunsmoke and sudden death dominate this chapter, it is worth looking at the hierarchy of lawmen in the West for the especial benefit of non-American readers puzzled by the difference between marshals and sheriffs. US marshals were first appointed in 1789 and their role in the West has been magnified by the movies. Their post was a Presidential appointment needing confirmation by the Senate and they were given states or territories to oversee. In fact, the deputies they were allowed to appoint were the ones who worked with local lawmen, indeed they were often already peace officers. Naturally, they were mainly concerned with Federal crimes, including those committed on Indian reservations, and they also had to do what they could to track down Army deserters.

There were also the locally appointed town marshals. A marshal was the Chief of Police and had a number of deputies to assist him. Apart from occasional shoot-outs, there were plenty of more mundane tasks, from keeping an eye on brothels to shooting stray dogs for a modest fee. Meanwhile, each county had a sheriff, normally elected for two years. Again, the under-sheriff and his deputies did most of the routine work.

Only a handful of these lawmen made a career of their jobs, those who did – and managed to survive for a number of years – becoming first rate professionals, like William 'Bill' Tilghman. Pay was rarely high. It was only the very fortunate sheriff who got as much as $500 a month and his underlings got far less: an under-sheriff usually got half his boss's salary, which might be half $200 a month, while deputies got around two-thirds of the under-sheriff's pay.

One thing needs stressing. These men, brilliant or obtuse, honest or corrupt, could expect help from their fellow townspeople. This will come as no surprise to readers who have noted the valiant behaviour of the people of Northfield and Coffeyville, but it has to be stressed because that admittedly magnificent Western *High Noon* gave a totally different impression. For dramatic reasons, but not historical ones, Gary Cooper was left on his own (until his Quaker wife came to his aid!).

The most famous stage for confrontations between lawmen and badmen was the Kansas cowtown. Abilene, Dodge City and the rest were famous in their own day and are now part of the mythology of countless millions who know them from films and television.

The cowtowns sprang into being to satisfy an urgent need. In the summer of 1865, thousands of defeated Texans returned home to find their ranches in ruins and vast numbers of unbranded cattle running wild. Before the war the cattle industry was prospering in Texas, with drives to New Orleans, north to Missouri along the Shawnee Trail, and even as far as California and Oregon. The cattle were longhorns, the mean, moody, hard-hided descendants of animals brought from Spain to the New World, and after the war there was not much market for them locally.

As the ranchers and their cowboys – who worked for around $30 a month – set about rounding up stock and rebuilding their property, they heard that in the north and east steers were worth $50 a head. But though a trail was blazed to the mining camps of Colorado by Charlie Goodnight and Oliver Loving in 1866, herds trying to reach the Midwestern settlements kept running into trouble. Outlaw bands, many of them staffed with murderous ex-guerillas, were a constant hazard, Indians a lesser one, as many were from the Five Civilized Tribes, driven westwards into Indian Territory a generation earlier. They were mainly content with toll money. But the farmers of Missouri and eastern Kansas objected to the longhorns because they carried tick fever northwards, though immune themselves to the deadly disease.

At this bleak moment a thirty-year-old cattle dealer from Illinois, Joseph McCoy, appeared. He was a born organiser, a visionary and the saviour of the Texans, for he saw the need of a trail beyond the irate farmers, and also decided to attempt to swing the cattle trade from St. Louis, Missouri, to Chicago. He searched for a place on the railroad that would make a good shipping

above
Joseph G. McCoy, whose transformation of a tiny hamlet into the cowtown of Abilene had a decisive effect on the Texas cattle industry.

opposite, above
Texas cowboys who went up the trail in 1866 were liable to be flogged and robbed by roving bands of Northern ex-guerillas.

opposite, below
Stampede! The only hope for cowboys when a stampede occurred was to try and get the thundering Longhorns into a circle.

point and found a tiny hamlet, whose liveliest spot was a thriving prairie dog colony in its main street. It was on the Union Pacific Eastern Division Railway and under his guidance it soon had a large siding to take a hundred cattle cars at a time, also vast pens and corrals. On 5 September 1867, the first shipment of longhorns set out for the stockyards of Chicago from this growing town surrounded by good grassland and with plenty of water. Its name was Abilene.

There had been cowtowns of a sort before Abilene, of course, but this was the first famous one, and the one that set the pattern for most of those that were to follow it. Not only did the railroad pass through the middle of town, but the rails rigidly divided the residential and business parts of Abilene from the 'wrong side of the tracks' where the Texas cowboys were to be found patronising the saloons, brothels, gambling dens and dance halls, or combinations of all of them.

The cowboys came up the Chisholm Trail, named for a Scottish-Cherokee trader, Jesse Chisholm. Abilene was reached by a branch off the main trail known as McCoy's

Extension. A few thousand longhorns came up the trail in 1867, but in 1871, the boom year, no less than 600,000 reached Abilene. There were to be other trails – and other cowtowns, notably Wichita, Ellsworth, Caldwell and Dodge City.

The Texans, who included a number of Mexican vaqueros and some blacks, arrived in town in need of amusement. They had endured a 1,000-mile journey which was rugged enough even if natural or man-made disasters had not occurred. After a cowboy hit town and enjoyed a bath and climbed into new clothes – the old ones were filthy and verminous by now – he wanted some action and, until law and order of a sort came to the cowtowns, that was likely to include shooting up a town for the sheer hell of it. A lawman might be chased out of it or worse if he was a weakling, and the fact that many lawmen were Northerners did not make them any more popular with Confederate veterans. Naturally, the average cowboy was no match for a professional gunfighter, lawman or otherwise, but drunken Texans with pistols could menace the more sober citizens.

The Texas cowboy, for all his bias against Mexicans, Indians, sheep, sheepmen, and Northern lawmen, and his resentment that he depended on Northern money and cattle buyers, was a hard-working man, loyal to his boss and comrades and respectful to women, but the inhabitants of the cowtowns, even those joyfully making money out of him and his friends, could hardly be expected to appreciate his better qualities. Typical of local feelings is this extract from the Topeka *Daily Commonwealth* of 15 August 1871:

> His diet is principally Navy plug and whisky, and the occupation of his heart is gambling. His dress consists of a flannel shirt with a handkerchief encircling his neck, butternut pants, and a pair of long boots in which are always to be found the legs of his pants. His head is covered with a sombrero, which is a Mexican hat with a low crown and a brim of mammoth dimensions. He generally wears a revolver on each side, which he will use with as little hesitation on a man as on a wild animal. Such a character is dangerous and desperate, and each one generally has killed his man. There are good and even honorable men among them, but run-away boys and men who find it too hot for them even in Texas join the cattle drovers and constitute a large proportion of them. They drink, swear, and fight; and life with them is a round of boisterous gaiety and indulgence in sensual pleasure.

The 'sensual pleasure' to be had from the local 'sisters in sin' belongs to Chapter Six. But the prostitutes, along with the card sharps and pimps, all helped form the background against which the cowtown marshals and their deputies worked. One can sympathise with the citizens made prosperous by Texan money, some stating that the towns should be made respectable, others pointing out that the Texans would more than somewhat resent such a thing. Finally a compromise was made: 'illegal' establishments were allowed to stay open but fined heavily enough to help make the towns prosper still more.

And prosper they did, some for a season or two, one, Dodge City, for many years – from the early 1870s until 1885, when Kansas banned the trail-cattle industry, and Dodge, like other cowtowns before it, changed its ways.

By then many lawmen had become legends in and outside Kansas.

Back in 1867, there had been little trouble in Abilene, but it was evident that things would soon be livening up. They did: by 1869 it was virtually a Texan town. One old-timer later recalled: 'When you heard one or two shots, you waited breathlessly for a third. A third shot meant a death on Texas Street.'

The situation for respectable citizens was grim. When some of the citizens were spurred into fighting the cowboys, the Texans proceeded to set fire to parts of the town and shoot at passers by. They destroyed a new jail, scared women and children and rode into saloons. This was the Wild West with a vengeance.

Not until June 1870, by which time the desperate citizens had managed to have Abilene made a third-class city and therefore have

above
'He liked them filled right up!' the boys told the bartender.

opposite, above
Cowboys at Abilene, Kansas, but the train carries passengers, not cattle.

opposite, below
Whooping it up, cowboy style. Note the Chinaman. The Chinese came to America seeking gold. Many later helped build the Central Pacific Railroad. They often suffered in the West because of their habit of wearing pigtails.

the right to hold elections, did a marshal appear on the streets. He was an exceptional man, and much of what we know about his time in Abilene we owe to T. C. Henry, the then mayor, who delivered a notable eulogy when a memorial stone to him was unveiled in Abilene's cemetery in 1904. His name was Tom Smith.

It was Henry who hired the big, handsome lawman, whose early life is somewhat obscure. He was probably a New Yorker of Irish parentage who became a policeman, then left the force for some reason. Unless anyone proves otherwise, he was the 'Bear River' Tom Smith who acted as a railroad troubleshooter at tough 'end-of-track' shanty towns where every kind of shark endeavoured to lift hard-earned wages from the workers. He earned his title at Bear River, Wyoming, when he led a gang of workers against townspeople who had thrown some of their comrades into jail. Lawman Billy Breakenridge met him later at Kit Carson, Colorado, and dubbed him the bravest man he had ever met, 'always neatly dressed, and very quiet and gentlemanly'. Breakenridge noted that Smith rarely carried a gun and depended on strength

and ability for making arrests, and he quoted a remarkable statement by Smith after he had dealt with a bully – 'Anyone can bring in a dead man, but to my way of thinking a good officer is the one that brings them in alive.'

It was this admirable man who presented himself to T. C. Henry. Smith's fighting reputation did not go down well with Henry's colleagues and he failed to get elected, but he was hastily summoned back when local lawmen failed miserably to curb the Texans.

Smith looked around the town and said he would take the job. 'I will stop their carrying firearms,' said Tom. 'You see we could stand guns or whiskey, but we can't stand both. There's no chance to stop the whiskey and we might as well stop the guns. Then there will be less danger.'

As Smith said: '[You may] as well contend with a frenzied maniac as

above
T. C. Henry, Abilene's first mayor.

above, right
Tom Smith, marshal of Abilene, who tamed the town with his sledgehammer fists, a weapon that the Texans neither understood nor appreciated.

opposite
Deprived of drink on their ranches and on the trail, cowboys often went wild in the cowtowns, especially after taking rot-gut whiskey on board. But even when sober, high spirits could turn sour.

an armed and drunken cowboy', then he was sworn in and left Henry who 'watched him with misgivings'.

Almost immediately, Tom ran into trouble in the shape of Big Hank Hawkins whose hobby was making things lively for lawmen. Nobody could disarm him and live was his boast.

He asked if Smith was the man who was going to run the town. Smith told him that he was now marshal and was going to enforce the law, including the ban on wearing guns. 'I shall be obliged,' he said politely, 'to trouble you for those guns which you have in your belt.'

'I will not give them up to any live man,' rasped Big Hank.

The duologue continued until the moment came when Big Hank told Smith that if he wanted his guns he could try and take them, then dropped his hand to his pistol. But before he could reach it, Tom Smith stepped in and sent him sprawling with a savage uppercut, then bent down and took the guns.

'I will give you ten seconds to start for the city limits and get out of range,' he said and Big Hank slunk hastily away.

A crony of Big Hank's, Wyoming Frank, heard the news and spread it abroad that he was going after the new marshal. The pair met that Sunday morning outside the Texas House on Texas Street, the heartland of the cowboys.

Frank asked Tom Smith if he was the right man, having opened his coat to show a .44. Smith admitted his identity and said, politely as always: 'I see that you carry a gun contrary to the law and I must request that you give it to me.' He then stepped towards Wyoming Frank, who started backing away into a saloon.

Tom Smith followed and stepped so near him that he could not draw his gun. Back went Wyoming Frank and forward went Tom Smith until the former was lodged against the bar, then Smith asked once again: 'Will you give me that gun?'

'Come and take it if you can!' Wyoming Frank challenged him and Smith loosed a tremendous right to his jaw which half turned him round, then followed it up with an equally strong blow with his left to the back of Frank's ear. Seconds later, he found himself lying on the floor, face downwards.

'With lightning rapidity the marshal secured his gun, and, with it, heavily beat the prostrate desperado over that part of his anatomy usually used in propelling bums out of a saloon,' recalled Henry, who was watching the scene with some pride.

Smith swung round on his impressed Sunday congregation and said: 'I am city marshal of this town . . . I shall treat everybody fairly and respectfully, but I want it distinctly understood that no guns will be carried except by those authorised by law to carry them. I shall take all weapons to the mayor's office, and when owners are ready to leave town they can call there and get them.' Then he returned to Wyoming Frank, and gave him five minutes to get out of town – and stay out.

Tom Smith headed for the door, but before he got there the barman came over with his own gun and said: 'That was the nerviest act I ever saw. You did your duty, and that coward got what he deserved. Here is my gun. I reckon I'll not need it so long as you are marshal of this town.'

Then everyone volunteered his pistol and gunbelt.

'Hand your guns to the bartender to keep until you want to go out of camp,' Smith told them all, or, as the average western has it: 'Park yer shootin' irons on the bar.' Tom Smith had tamed wild and woolly Abilene in two days flat.

For all that long summer Tom Smith kept his brand of peace in Abilene, whose city fathers had the good sense and manners to pay him well. He was made deputy US marshal of Dickinson County, but his main beat was the town, which he patrolled on his grey stallion Silverheels. The sight of him and his already legendary reputation was enough to deter most Texans, even the foolhardiest, but the riding had an extra advantage. Smith always said that a man on a moving horse was harder for a drunk to hit than a lone figure patrolling the streets on foot. Proof of his theory was provided on the three occasions when bullets failed to hit him.

Only once did Tom Smith's luck nearly run out in Abilene itself. Hearing shots coming from the Old Fruit Saloon, he dismounted and entered the long, narrow building through its only door. At the far end was a drunken Texan, brandishing a pistol and Smith began walking towards him. Too late he realised he had been trapped, as the other cowboys cut off his retreat. But he reached their drunken friend and squared up to him.

There was a pause, as if Tom Smith's legendary reputation had the Texans uncertain as how to act. The marshal acted first, drawing one of his two pearl-handled Colts and bringing the barrel crashing against the drunk's jaw. He fell to the floor.

Then all hell was let loose, with a cowboy at the back trying to kill Tom Smith but hitting two of the Texans instead, while others shot their pistols in the air. A kerosene lamp was hurled at the marshal, landing beside him, but failing to explode. The action caused a panic as some weeks earlier a lamp had exploded in a saloon and men had been burnt to death. Not wishing to repeat history, the Texans headed for the door.

Amidst the uproar, Tom Smith picked up the still unconscious cowboy, got him across his shoulder and walked out of the building, heading for his office. None of the Texans dared shoot him in case they hit their still slumbering comrade.

The story of Thomas James Smith, 'Bear River' Tom Smith, the quiet, polite, valiant lawman, whom many believed had started his professional life as a New York cop, had a tragic ending. It was an ironic one, for having survived and triumphed in Abilene's busiest season yet, he was murdered, not by cowboys but by two settlers in November outside the city limits; indeed he was all but decapitated. He had been asked by County Sheriff Cramer, then a dying man, to arrest one Andrew McConnell, who was charged with the murder of a settler. Taking his deputy, Jim McDonald, with him, Smith reached McConnell's dugout and told him he was under arrest. McConnell shot him in the chest, but Smith came to grips with him and, despite his wound, had overpowered him, when a neighbour, Moses Miles, came up from behind with an axe.

Abilene citizens despised deputy McDonald forever after the tragedy for failing to save his chief, but it seems that he finally sprang into

action and shot off two of Miles's fingers before the murderers made their getaway, then rode off to town for help. The killers were caught by a posse but to the fury of Abilene got a prison sentence instead of the hanging that everyone felt they so richly deserved.

Tom Smith's funeral was the greatest that Abilene has ever seen, with every place of business closed, black crepe in every window, and even some of the saloons in Texas Street closed as a mark of respect. 'Behind the hearse', recalled old-timer Stuart Henry later, 'walked the dead marshal's iron-grey horse Silverheels, saddled and bridled as he had left it. Tom's pearl-handled brace of revolvers, presented to him by the community, hung in their holsters from the pommel.' The *Chronicle* said of him: 'He was a stranger to fear, and yet in the private walks of life a most diffident man . . .' And when the memorial to the story book marshal was dedicated in 1904, the following inscription was placed on the plaque:

THOMAS J. SMITH
Marshal of Abilene, 1870
Died, a Martyr to duty,
Nov. 2, 1870
A fearless hero of Frontier Days
Who in Cowboy chaos
Established the supremacy of
the law.

above
Gambling in Cheyenne, Wyoming, in 1877.

left
A bar-room brawl. Shoot-outs were liable to occur at very short range.

opposite, above
Broadway, Abilene, Kansas, in 1875.

opposite, below
'Rowdy Joe' Lowe, a Kansas gambler, gunfighter and brothel-keeper, married to 'Rowdy Kate'.

Of course, the City Council of Abilene could not hope to find another Tom Smith, but they hired in his place one of the most famous men in the West, a man who more than a century after his death remains perhaps the most famous gunfighter of all. His name was James Butler Hickok, the legendary 'Wild Bill'. In Abilene he used not sledgehammer fists, but six-guns: with his reputation he had no choice. And in his different way he, too, as we shall see, was a fine law officer.

Born at Homer, Illinois in 1837, Wild Bill was to be credited with more than a hundred killings, thanks to rumour and his own Frontier habit of gross exaggeration: he told the great explorer, H. M. Stanley, when the Welsh-American dynamo was a young reporter: 'I would be willing to take my oath on the Bible tomorrow that I have killed over a hundred, a long ways off . . . I never killed one man without good cause.' An admiring Stanley lapped it all up, but Hickok's best biographer, Joseph G. Rosa, has reduced the number of substantiated slayings to seven!

Young Hickok went to Kansas in 1856 to buy farming land for the family and found himself involved in the Border wars. Successively, he was a constable at Montecello Township, a stagecoach driver and in the Civil War – in which he was on the Northern side – a wagon-master, scout, courier and spy. Afterwards, he was an army scout in Kansas and Colorado (where he met Stanley). Before concentrating on his notorious season in Abilene, our main concern, it should be noted that while acting sheriff of Ellis County, Kansas, he killed two men in Hays. He lost his job in the next election, but returned to Hays in July 1870 to see some friends. In a saloon he was set upon by some drunken troopers of Custer's Seventh Cavalry. The circumstances are disputed, but not the result. Hickok shot two soldiers, one of them dying, and he had to leave fast to escape from vengeful comrades of the dead man.

Custer's wife Libbie has left us one of the most vivid accounts of Wild Bill:

Physically, he was a delight to look upon. Tall, lithe, and free in every motion, he rode and walked as if every muscle was perfection, and the careless swing of his body as he moved seemed perfectly in keeping with the man, the country, the time in which he lived.

Hickok's eight month reign in Abilene came at a time when his reputation as a 'pistoleer' was unequalled in the West. Tom Smith had baffled the Texans as well as awed them, but Hickok's methods were more conventional. No longer in buckskins, but fashionably dressed, with twin Colt Navy revolvers stuck in his belt, their butts forward, he was a man not to be tangled with in fair fight. Cursed with his extreme reputation, he rightly took care of himself, avoiding bright lights and dark alleyways, and he survived in what was Abilene's greatest and final season as a cowtown.

The most controversial incident that summer was a gunfight worlds away from the formal one at Springfield, Missouri, to be described in Chapter Five. It happened on the night of 5 October when the season was almost over. A number of Texans were still in town, however, bent on visiting the County Fair before returning home. On the evening of the 5th, Hickok noted some fifty Texans whooping it up in the saloons. Some, he was told, were forcing people to buy them drinks, citizens being forcibly carried into the saloons for the honour of treating Texans. Hickok himself, according to one story, treated some Texans when they agreed to behave themselves properly and keep their hands off their guns.

Around 9 pm he was enjoying a farewell drink in the Novelty Bar with a close friend, Mike Williams, who that summer had worked in the saloons and had just finished a spell as a bouncer at the stage door of the Novelty Theatre.

Suddenly, a shot rang out from outside the Alamo Saloon and Hickok left after telling Mike Williams to stay put. He entered the Alamo by the rear entrance and swiftly walked to its elaborate glass front doors. There stood a crowd of armed Texans, headed by a gambler, Philip Coe, even taller than Hickok and with a pistol in his hand.

'Who fired that shot?' demanded Wild Bill, and Coe said that he had fired it – at a dog. As Hickok had been told that Coe intended to kill him 'before the frost', the dog story seemed unconvincing.

There was a longish story of tension between the two and even a rumour that they had fought over the favours of a prostitute. Now they faced each other and Hickok was furious, as the Texans were openly defying the city's edict against firearms. He ordered them all to disarm and quit town, Coe choosing that moment to point his gun at the marshal. 'As quick as thought,' reported the press, Wild Bill pulled his 'Navies' and fired at Coe, but just as he pulled the triggers of the Colts someone came between the two men. The unfortunate intruder was hit by both balls and, dropping his own gun, he fell into the street.

Coe got off two shots, one of them going between Wild Bill's legs and hitting the ground, the other piercing his coat tail. Hickok fired two more shots at Coe, both hitting his stomach.

One of the badly wounded Coe's shots seems to have hit an onlooker and Hickok swung round as the man was falling and shouted: 'If any of you want the balance of these pills, come and get them!'

The Texans were turned to stone as Hickok continued: 'Now every one of you mount his pony and ride for his camp and do it damn quick!' and a few minutes later there was hardly a soul in sight.

Hickok looked at the men he had shot. Coe was mortally wounded and lingered on several agonising days. To Hickok's horror the other man, who was already dead, was his friend Mike Williams.

Hickok, tears running down his face, carried the body into the Alamo, where he laid it on a billard table. He had killed what had seemed a potential enemy and an armed one, and the fact that it was Williams drove him berserk. He rushed through every saloon left open in Abilene and cleared everybody he found out of them. Soon, the area on the wrong side of the tracks was like a ghost town.

Hickok had his friend's body shipped back to Kansas City and he paid for his funeral. Meanwhile, the Texas version of the affair, with Wild Bill shooting Coe in the back, was spread abroad, though the coroner's report upheld what might be called the Kansas version. The local press had no doubt that the affair was a further example of Hickok's town-taming ability, but the episode was yet another reason for the citizens wanting to terminate their association with the cattle trade, however lucrative it might be to them. The Texans were asked to take their cattle somewhere else in 1872.

Hickok was not sacked, as some stated, over the Mike Williams incident, but simply because Abilene no longer needed the expensive luxury of a top lawman. Naturally, there had been those who disliked

opposite
The men who tried to rob the Medicine Lodge Bank, Kansas. Gang leader Marshal Henry Newton Brown is second from left.

right
Ellsworth, Kansas. The drovers were the bosses, not the cowboys.

below, right
Billy Thompson was Ben Thompson's kid brother. When Billy committed a despicable murder, Ben, though enraged, saved him from the punishment he deserved.

his methods compared with Smith's, but the *Chronicle* must have spoken for the majority who understood the facts about policing a cowtown when it stated: 'We think he is entitled to the thanks of law-abiding citizens throughout the State for the safety of life and property in Abilene, which has been secured, more through his daring, than any other agency.'

Before seeing where the trade went, the rest of Hickok's short life may be briefly told. After visits to friends and acquaintances in the West, he embarked on a rather absurd career as an actor with his friend Buffalo Bill Cody, who had not yet started his immortal Wild West show, but was running a Combination presenting Western dramas to Eastern audiences. Hickok was a reluctant recruit and escaped in March 1874 after just over six months' Thespian activity. His best bit of acting was spontaneous. The plot demanded that a whiskey bottle should pass between two scouts and himself – as Himself – the 'whiskey' being tea. Wild Bill took a great swig from the bottle, then his expression gradually changed from joy to stark horror. Spewing a mouthful of the beverage towards the wings, he roared: 'Cold tea don't count – either I get real whiskey or I ain't tellin' no story!' The applause was immense.

He returned to the West and married a circus proprietor called Agnes Lake Thatcher in March 1876, then, leaving his bride with some relatives, headed for Deadwood in the Black Hills. There on 2 August 1876, just a week after his friend Custer's Last Stand, he was shot through the back of the head by a hired assassin named Jack McCall while he was playing cards. A miners' jury, which may have been bribed, set the murderer free, but on 1 March 1877 he was hanged after a legal trial. Wild Bill's body lies in a beautiful cemetery above Deadwood and just behind it lies Calamity Jane's, to be featured in Chapter Six, who liked to claim that she and Hickok were lovers/husband and wife, whereas, except in the near proximity of death, she appears to have had far less to do with him than any other Frontier gal linked with his name. But both of them are now part of the pantheon of Western mythology, the difference being that Wild Bill Hickok deserves his place as one of the few white men that even those who care nothing for the West have heard of. And the others? His good friends George Armstrong Custer and Buffalo Bill Cody, and those legendary badmen, Jesse James and Billy the Kid.

In July 1871, the Santa Fe Railway reached Newton, which was soon a very lively spot. A writer in the Wichita *Tribune* stated:

> I have been in a good many towns but Newton is the fastest one I have ever seen. Here you may see young girls not over sixteen drinking whisky, smoking cigars, cursing and swearing until one almost loses the respect they should have for the weaker sex. I heard one of their townsmen say that he didn't believe there were a dozen virtuous women in town. This speaks well for a town of 1,500 inhabitants. He further told me if I had any money that I would not be safe with it here. It is a common expression that they have a man every morning for breakfast.

Ben Thompson, a gunfighter from Yorkshire, was also a soldier and a gambler. He was murdered in San Antonio in 1884.

In this liberated cowtown there were soon twenty-seven saloons, and an area called 'Hide Park' was the haunt of prostitutes and their clients. Its most notorious shoot-out was a community one, so much so that it became known as the 'Newton General Massacre'. Space does not permit a full account of the event, but it began when an ex-lawman with an evil reputation, Mike McCluskie, returned to Newton despite the fact that Texans had threatened his life after one of their friends had been killed. McCluskie was holding court in Perry Tutle's saloon when a group of Texans, led by Hugh Anderson, came in and went up to him.

'You are a cowardly son of a bitch,' Anderson told McCluskie, while the other Texans took up strategic positions. 'I will blow the top of your head off!' And he opened fire.

McCluskie was hit in the neck, but he staggered up and fired his pistol, which failed to act as the hammer did not detonate the cap. By the time he had recocked it, he was a mass of blood and, as he collapsed, Anderson shot him through his back.

For once the cliche 'all hell was let loose' is the sober truth, for it seemed that everyone started firing, and the saloon was soon full of smoke. Then a stranger came in, a youthful gunfighter who began blazing away at the cowboys, several of whom died. From all over town men and women rushed to the scene as screams and shouts rent the air, then it was all over. And when the smoke had faded away everyone looked for the 'Avenging Nemesis' who had burst in to scourge the killer cowboys.

He had vanished, and no one ever knew for certain who he was. But some months later, in a poem about the bloody fracas, Theodore F. Price related that the mysterious youth was a man named Riley who had once been befriended by McCluskie, then, having failed to save him, avenged him. It was claimed that Riley was dying of tuberculosis. Fact or fiction, the result was the same: the citizens decided it was high time to employ lawmen of a better quality than McCluskie, though their best choice, James H. McDonald, who had been Tom Smith's deputy, did not stay with them long. Perhaps more fascinating is the aftermath to the massacre, for three years later a man said to be McCluskie's brother fought Hugh Anderson at Medicine Lodge, Kansas. When both had drilled each other with bullet holes, they crawled up to each other and proceeded to stab one another to death.

The cowtown of Caldwell lost its apparently exemplary marshal in the most unexpected way. His name

left
Wichita, Kansas, in 1870, not long before it became a wild and booming cowtown.

below
The railroad reached Wichita in 1872 and the town enjoyed a three-year cattle boom. Things quietened down after the trade passed to Dodge City. This peaceful picture was taken in 1878.

was Henry Newton Brown and the Caldwell *Post* noted in July 1882 that the new assistant marshal – as he was then – was said to be one of the quickest men on the trigger in the Southwest. By late December he was marshal and on New Year's Day, 1883, the citizens gave him a rifle as a present. Little did they know that their lawman had quite a past behind him, including violent service in the Lincoln County War, but if they had, would it have mattered? Their paragon neither drank, gambled, smoked nor chewed tobacco, and he married a local girl.

So it came as a shock when in May, 1884, their marshal went spectacularly to the bad, along with three others, all of whom descended on Medicine Lodge to rob its bank.

It was an ill-planned affair. The gang had never indulged in bank robbery, they had not reconnoitred properly, and though they murdered the bank's president and cashier, the latter managed to lock the bank vault before he died, leaving the would-be robbers empty handed.

A posse captured them and they were placed in the Medicine Lodge jail, but that night a mob broke in. The sheriff and his deputies were overpowered and their prisoners tried to escape. Brown was shot dead by buckshot and bullets before he had got far, the other three were strung up later that night. As for the people of Caldwell, it took some time to believe the awful facts, and the editor of the local *Journal*, though he could not deny them, was only able to dredge up one flaw in Brown's behaviour as marshal: 'He was too ready to use his revolver or Winchester.' Quick on the trigger he may have been, but he was the best lawman Caldwell ever had. No one knows why he suddenly reverted to crime. Perhaps he just wanted more money.

The most sensational event in Ellsworth's history never occurred outside the pages of Stuart Lake's semi-fictional paean of praise to a controversial lawman of the second rank, Wyatt Earp, whom he virtually canonised and had win much of the West single-handed. The book is variously known as *He Carried a Six-Shooter* or *Wyatt Earp, Frontier Marshal*, and readers will recall how Wyatt Earp, then unknown, stepped forward to arrest the great Ben Thompson, who was backed up by a hundred or more drunken Texans. Our Hero succeeded, but, alas, there is no contemporary evidence that this incomparable feat ever happened.

Plenty did happen in Ellsworth, however, much of it centred round

right
Bat Masterson, the most famous member of his family, was born in Canada. A renowned lawman and gunfighter, he finished life as a New York sports reporter.

below
Jim Masterson, marshal of Dodge City from 1879 to 1881, and one of three brothers to serve on the city's police force.

opposite
Billy Brooks ran the gamut from stagecoach driver to lawman and, lastly, horse-thief. He was lynched in 1874.

Ben Thompson, a Yorkshire born gunfighter who fought with the Second Texas Cavalry in the Civil War, then served, like other Southerners, with the Emperor Maximilian in Mexico. Gambling became his main interest after Maximilian's death, but his trigger-nometry was superb, no less a judge than Bat Masterson considering him a master of the art.

Ben had a brother Billy who was rather a trial to him. Billy was arrested by Edward Hogue after he had fired a pistol on the street on 11 June 1873, and was fined. Ben, who had arrived in Ellsworth to start a saloon, could have done without the publicity, but decided that saloonkeeping was less to his taste than gambling.

The season of 1873 was a poor one for the cattle business, and that, plus the heat, soured tempers in the town, the Texans' chief enemy being an unpleasant gunfighter, John 'Happy Jack' Morco who, on being released after an arrest for vagrancy, was made a lawman on the local force. Morco enjoyed running Texans in and charged Billy Thompson with assault with a pistol. Again, Billy was fined. On 15 August Ben Thompson, who had staked a fellow gambler, John Sterling, the terms being that if the latter won, Ben would get half, was furious when his partner vanished with $1,000. He tracked him to Nick Lenz's saloon and, on asking him for his cut, was slapped in the face. At this electric moment John Morco leapt between the pair, drew his revolver, and forced Ben to leave.

He made for Brennan's saloon where he was told that Sterling and 'Happy Jack' were armed and waiting for him, so he ran to Jack New's saloon for his weapons.

Billy suddenly appeared carrying Ben's British-made shotgun and the two Thompsons made for the street, Billy being the worse for drink. As he staggered along, he discharged a hail of buckshot from one of his brother's shotgun barrels, which drove two Texans off the street. Meanwhile, Ben led the way to the railroad where they could get down to serious fighting without the risk of hitting bystanders.

News of the incidents had been brought to Sheriff Chauncey Whitney, an ex-soldier and scout, who raced to the brothers and tried to avert a fight; indeed, he got them back to Brennan's saloon. Then someone called that Morco was coming with a gun and Ben ran out and fired. Morco dodged into a store.

Out of the saloon dashed Billy with Whitney behind him, then Billy swung round and aimed the shotgun at Whitney. 'Don't shoot!' pleaded the lawman, backing away, but the drunken Billy pulled the trigger and Whitney screamed in agony.

'You've shot Whitney, our best friend!' raged Ben at his brother.

'I don't give a damn, and would have shot him even if he had been Jesus Christ,' muttered the wretched Billy.

Blood will out and Ben pushed Billy towards a horse, which he mounted and rode out of town, leaving Ben to face the enraged onlookers. He held them off for an hour, only surrendering to Hogue when it was agreed that Morco, too, should be disarmed.

It took Whitney three days to die. Throughout his agony he stated that Billy had shot him by accident. Not until 1877 was Billy brought to trial, but – perhaps because the jury was bribed, as some claimed – he was acquitted. As for Ben, he later became the colourful marshal of Austin, Texas, where his reputation made the crime figures drop significantly. True, he enjoyed getting drunk and shooting at street lamps, but the townspeople didn't mind his little ways until a gun battle with an old enemy in San Antonio made them sadly allow him to retire. Finally, Yorkshire's own gunfighter followed his many victims to the grave when he was murdered in 1884.

Wichita came into its own as a cowtown in 1872, when the railroad

arrived. The next year Michael Meagher was hired as marshal and, apart from a short break in 1874–5, kept the booming town reasonably peaceful for five years. When Wichita's position as a cowtown gave way to Caldwell, Meagher went there and was killed in a gunfight in 1881, not long before Henry Newton Brown arrived to make his name, then to lose it spectacularly at Medicine Lodge.

Meagher's qualities were much praised by the Wichita *Eagle*, not least because everyone knew how less peaceful things had been in his period out of office, when William Smith let the Texans dominate all Wichita. William 'Hurricane Bill' Martin and the 'Texas Gang' were shooting the place up when somebody rang the police alarm. At once, citizens grabbed every weapon they could find and rushed on to the street, some fifty of them confronting the Texans. Smith ran to the scene but had not the authority to get either side to back down.

There followed a remarkable scene (not starring Wyatt Earp, though Earp did do an efficient stint as a policeman in 1875 and part of 1876). S. M. Tucker, a lawyer, announced that he did not intend to waste his time. Did the marshal want anyone arrested, and if so, whom? Smith indicated the alarming figure of 'Hurricane Bill'.

Tucker cocked his shotgun and pointed it meaningfully at Bill's stomach, then commanded: 'Drop those guns!'

Bill knew he had met his match, so he shrugged his shoulders and announced: 'I guess you can have me.' Like lambs, the rest of his men followed their leader and were marched to jail.

In 1874, Dodge City became the 'Queen of the Cowtowns', though not until 1876 did she get her first official marshal, Lawrence E. Deger. A year later Edward J. Masterson replaced him just when his younger brother William 'Bat' Masterson was sheriff of Ford County. Brother Jim later joined the Dodge City force.

Ed Masterson was an excellent officer with a deservedly high reputation, but less than a year later, on 9 April 1878, tragedy struck. He had disarmed a Texan, Jack Wagner, handing his gun to A. M. Walker, Wagner's boss. Later, Ed, now with deputy marshal Nat Hayward, came across Wagner, who was armed once again, and drunk. Ed prepared to disarm him, while Wagner's cronies, also the worse for liquor, erupted from the nearest saloon. Deputy Hayward moved forward to support his boss but was halted by two Texans who threatened to kill him if he joined in, and one of the pair, thought to be Walker, pulled his trigger. Fortunately, the gun misfired. Simultaneously, Walker shot Ed Masterson in the stomach, the flame from the black powder at short range setting the marshal's clothes on fire. But the valiant Ed still managed to hit Wagner in the bowels, also badly damaging Walker.

above, right
David 'Mysterious Dave' Mather, a shadowy figure who operated on both sides of the law and who was reputed to be a 'very wicked man, a killer of killers' by Robert Wright of Dodge City.

right
Front Street, Dodge City, the Queen of the Cowtowns, as it was in 1878.

left
James 'Dog' Kelley (left), mayor of Dodge City, and Charles Hungerford. The odd nickname arose because the mayor kept greyhounds that had belonged to General Custer.

top
The interior of the Long Branch Saloon in Dodge City in the 1880s.

above
The Varieties Dance Hall at Dodge City.

opposite
John King Fisher was a friend of Ben Thompson and was killed with him in 1884.

Men came running to their marshal's aid and the rest of the Texans were rapidly arrested. Meanwhile, Ed, refusing help despite his appalling wound, managed to make George Hoover's saloon on the far side of the street, and, swaying on his feet, told bartender George Hinkle: 'George, I'm shot!' Then he collapsed, dying half an hour later in his brother Bat's room. Bat was not involved in the fight according to contemporary reports, but was the only close relative at Ed's funeral the next day. 'A PUBLIC CALAMITY' the Ford County *Globe* rightly called the event, and the funeral showed just how much Ed Masterson had been respected in the town. Wagner only survived a day, the Dodge City *Times* stating that he had previously fallen from his horse and was thought to have been rendered partially insane. Walker recovered.

Brother Bat, born in 1853 in Canada and christened Bartholomew – though for an unknown reason he was later called William Barclay Masterson – was more fortunate, dying at the sports desk of a New York paper as late as 1921. He was one of the most likeable Western characters, credited, like so many more, with vast numbers of killings. He did nothing to set the record straight – it did no harm to give the opposition the idea that a lawman was a man-killer – though he was not in the Wild Bill Hickok league as a tall story-teller. But he was not averse to feeding false facts to reporters or letting others do so, as when a Dr Cockerell told the New York *Sun* how Bat had shot seven men dead within a few minutes, and later described how Bat had killed a Mexican father and son, put them in a sack, then failed to get the reward for killing them because a two days' ride and the hot sun 'swelled and disfigured the heads so that they were unrecognisable, taking advantage of which the authorities refused to pay the reward'.

Bat's career spanned all the more lively aspects of Frontier life, including Indian fighting, for he was in the battle at Adobe Wells in the Texas Panhandle in 1874 between some thirty-five buffalo hunters

above
The Dodge City Peace Commission were not a group of lawmen (though some of them had been). They were friends of gambler Luke Short, who came to Dodge to help him when he fell out with the city authorities. From left to right: (standing) W. H. Harris, Luke Short, Bat Masterson and W. F. Petillon, Dodge's champion pie-eater; (sitting) Charles Bassett, Wyatt Earp, M. F. McClain and Neil Brown.

right
Peace comes to Dodge City. A drugstore in 1887.

holed up in a minute hamlet and 500 or more Indians of the South Plains, an action that lasted for five days. He had made his name as a scout, buffalo hunter and gunfighter before he reached Dodge in 1877, where he managed to get himself arrested for helping a local 'character', Bobby Gill, escape from Marshal Larry Deger, who was marching him to jail. Presumably under the influence of drink, Bat took exception to the man-mountain marshal escorting tiny Bobby Gill. He got a pistol-whipping for his pains and was fined: it was, after all, rather embarrassing, as brother Ed was already the assistant marshal of Dodge City.

Bat made his name when, only two weeks after becoming sheriff of Ford County, he led the posse that was responsible for arresting most of a gang who had robbed a train thirty-five miles from Dodge, a dangerous assignment embarked on by two other groups of pursuers who never got near the criminals. Brave, quick-witted and charming, he ceased his job in 1880 and went on his travels, returning from time to time, and sometimes acting as a lawman elsewhere. As city marshal of the mining town of Creede, Colorado, one Lute Johnson paid him a fine tribute in the Denver *Republican* in 1892: 'Bat Masterson is generally regarded in the camp as the nerviest man of all the fighters here . . . all the thugs and toughs fear him as they do no other dozen men in camp. Let an incipient riot start and all that is necessary to quell it is the whisper, "There comes Masterson"'. Later, he married an actress, became a fight promoter, drank too much, ran up debts and, happily – as has been noted – found sense and security in New York City. We shall meet him again.

With the banning of the trail cattle industry in 1885, Dodge City's reign was over. No one knows how many perished in the cattle towns between 1867 and 1885, but it was certainly not the thousands that legend – and Westerns – suggest. In 1968, Robert Dykstra in his fine *The Cattle Towns* claimed that only forty-five killings occurred between 1870 and 1885 and only a few were directly caused by gunfights between lawmen and cowboys. But since then others have suggested that the total was far higher, especially in Dodge City and Newton. Yet far higher does not mean that the figure runs into hundreds. As for the cowtown marshals and their deputies, they deserve the fame that clings to them to this day. Their characters varied from admirable to questionable and downright bad, but the best of them replaced anarchy and sometimes terror with the rule of law.

The Texas Rangers

Of all the groups of lawmen on the Frontier, none had a more remarkable record of achievement over a long period than the Texas Rangers. The Mounties – then the North-West Mounted Police, founded in 1873 – were their equal, but had less dauntingly wild conditions to deal with, and had the benefit of scarlet coats that the Indians knew from past experience spelt justice and friendship. The Rangers remain controversial to this day, but their record in the time span of this book surely invites admiration tinged with astonishment. Every Texan knows – and makes sure that legions of Americans know – the story of the mayor in West Texas in the 1870s with a riot on his hands. 'Urgently need a company of rangers,' he telegraphed their headquarters in Austin.

Two days later a train arrived and out of it stepped a keen-eyed, youthful-looking man with a Winchester, a Colt and a bag. 'Where's the rest of 'em?' inquired the mayor, frowning anxiously.

'There's just me,' replied the man.

'I asked for a company,' gasped the mayor.

'Why so you did,' said the Ranger consolingly, 'but there's only one

Company E, Frontier Battalion, Texas Rangers, 1892.

right
Captain L. H. McNelly, one of the great figures in the history of the Texas Rangers.

below
Frederic Remington's fine impression of a Texas Ranger.

opposite
General Baylor (left) was a thoroughly bad Indian agent. With him is a legendary Texas Ranger of the early days before the Civil War, 'Big Foot' Wallace.

riot, ain't there?' 'One riot, one Ranger' is as much a part of Texas history as 'Remember the Alamo!'

The very first rangers were raised by the Mexicans in the 1820s to protect the newly arrived American settlers from the Comanches, the Lords of the South Plains, who resented the new arrivals with some justification. They were supreme horsemen, and enjoyed fighting – and kidnapping white women. A sergeant and fourteen men were raised to aid the settlers, and later, Stephen Austin, leader of the Anglo-American Texans, raised ten men he called rangers. Their numbers were increased and in the Texas Revolution of 1835–6 they were actually called Texas Rangers for the first time. They made their name under such legendary figures as Captain John 'Jack' Coffee Hays, and he and his men, with their brand new Colt five-shooters, became the scourge of Indians and white bad-men alike. Only 150 men were raised in 1835, and they had to provide their own horses, saddles and blankets and exist on $1.25 a day. Hays excelled in solo acts of daring, so much so that one chief, a Lipan Indian ally of the Texans, noted: 'Me and Blue Wing not afraid to go to hell together. Captain Jack, great brave, not afraid to go to hell by himself.'

After the Civil War, Texas suddenly found itself without Rangers. First the victorious Union Army was officially in charge of the Frontier, followed by the hated Texas State Police which, being composed chiefly of ex-slaves, spoke volumes for the liberalism of Governor F. J. Davis but hardly helped promote good feeling. Their activities were controversial, and the cry went up: 'Bring back the Rangers!' In 1874, they came back.

The Frontier Battalion was raised under Major John B. Jones to fight Indians and quell unending feuds, while the 'Special Force of

left
Sergeant James Gillett wrote a classic book about the Texas Rangers, *Six Years with the Texas Rangers*. He later became marshal of El Paso, then a rancher.

opposite, above
A rugged group of Texas Rangers, including John R. Hughes (bottom right), who was to become a legend in his lifetime.

opposite, below
Two Arizona Rangers, C. H. Farnsworth (left) and W. K. Foster.

Rangers' under Captain L. H. McNelly was deputed to suppress lawlessness along the border with Mexico. McNelly was a veteran – and an honourable one – of the notorious State Police. These two superb outfits brought meaning to the phrase 'The Rangers are coming!' They have kept on coming until our own day, a typical example of the rugged breed at its finest being Frank Hamer. He belonged both to the Frontier and the modern Rangers, and was disgracefully libelled in the admittedly brilliant film *Bonnie and Clyde* in the imaginary scene where the gang captured and photographed him, and, indeed, in the scene where the lethal pair were finally killed.

Hamer, like all Rangers, used his initiative, though few went as far as Sergeant James Gillett, who actually kidnapped a killer out of Mexico.

The wanted man was Enofre Baca, who after a killing slipped across the Rio Grande to safety in the town of Zaragoza. Gillett's commander, Captain Baylor, could not officially allow him to cross into Mexico, so the sergeant persuaded a young Texan, George Lloyd, to cross illegally with him and extract the killer, who had been reported to be serving in a store.

The pair reached the town to find few people about, and Gillett entered the store as Lloyd held his horse. Baca was measuring calico for an old lady and there were only two other customers.

Gillett marched over to him, whipped out his gun, and grabbed the killer by the collar. He pressed his gun to Baca's head and urged him out of the shop, leaving the old woman in a dead faint behind him. Baca was forced to mount behind Lloyd and the trio rode away as the onlookers came to life and gave the alarm. As the town's church bells pealed out, a posse assembled and started after the kidnappers.

Two miles on, Lloyd's horse began to flag and, suddenly, nine men began to close on them, firing low to avoid hitting Baca. The Rangers switched him to Gillett's horse and reached the Rio Grande. With a final hail of bullets cutting into the water, they made the far side safely, where Gillett raised his stetson and waved it at the furious Mexicans.

Captain Baylor was not amused, but let them off with a severe reprimand, sticking by his men when the telegrams began to flow between Mexico City and Washington. Yet Baca's guilt was never in doubt, besides which the pair of kidnappers were now heroes. Gillett later retired from the Rangers and became marshal of El Paso, then a prosperous rancher.

Arizona, too, had its Rangers, led at first by a rugged ex-cattleman, Captain Burton C. Mossman, commanding a mere fourteen men. Asked for his methods for dealing with cattle thieves, Mossman pointed out that if they came along easy, all would be well, if not, 'we can make pretty short work of them',

and noted that most of them led a dog's life in the mesquite shrub to keep away from the law. He considered they should thank him for giving them a chance to come in and take their medicine!

Pinkerton's Detectives

More controversial than these state and territorial rangers were Allan Pinkerton's men. Pinkerton, born in Scotland in 1819, emigrated to Illinois after, strangely, having been an agitator for reform. Yet his love of law and order stemmed partly from the crippling of his policeman father by a mob. In Illinois he helped runaway slaves, but was soon devoting himself to his new detective agency. His biggest early break was to uncover a plot to kill Lincoln just after the latter's election, and in the Civil War he started the North's secret service, his failing being to exaggerate the enemy's numbers. This was meat and drink to the Union commander, McClennan, who was notably loath to attack, and who was finally sacked by Lincoln. This caused Pinkerton's influence to wane, so he was not on hand when the President was assassinated. 'If only I had been there to protect him,' lamented Pinkerton with reason.

Pinkerton and his men smashed the Reno gang of train-robbers, though, as we have seen, their tactics against the James boys backfired when the disastrous attack on the James cabin took place. Despite this fiasco, their famous and history-making 'Rogues gallery' of photographs and details of criminals helped tame the outlaws of the West, the key office in Denver,

left
Scottish-born Allan Pinkerton, founder of the famous detective agency.

above
Wells Fargo was the principal transporter of gold and silver in the West. The firm – founded by Henry Wells and William Fargo – eventually owned the world's greatest stagecoach empire.

Colorado, being run for some years by the most valiant of all Pinkerton operatives, James McParland. He was the man who had infiltrated the murderous Molly Maguire terrorists in the Pennsylvania coalfields in the 1870s and lived to tell the tale and convict them. Denver was meant to be a more gentle assignment, as his health had cracked under the strain, especially of having to drink too much alcohol to make the Mollies feel he was not to be entrusted with killings.

There were other detectives at work in the West, most notably Wells Fargo and Union Pacific undercover men. One of the former's most famous operatives was James B. Hume, who finally tracked down 'Black Bart', a stagecoach robber who enjoyed writing poetry, did not kill his victims, and signed himself 'Black Bart the PO8'.

Black Bart's real name was Charles E. Boles, though his alias was Charles E. Bolton, apparently a mining man who regularly stayed at a certain San Francisco hotel. A handkerchief dropped at the scene of a crime, complete with a faint laundry mark, finally finished his career, but he was only given six years in San Quentin prison as he had never killed anyone and had returned the bulk of the loot he had stolen in such a gentlemanly and sometimes poetic way.

Judges

Few of the judges who sentenced the West's criminals are remembered today except by specialists, but two remain Frontier immortals – for different reasons.

The first of them, Roy Bean, seems amusing enough now, and certainly gave his admirers plenty

of laughs in his own day, but his victims, especially when he was in what might politely be called a capricious mood, can hardly have seen the joke.

Kentucky-born Bean – the event happened sometime in the late 1820s – had a lively life, some of it illegal, before leaving his wife and children in an area of San Antonio, Texas, that had become known as Beanville, to follow the Southern Pacific Railroad as it was extended westwards, and serve whiskey to the construction crews.

Bean soon dominated the roaring camps at end-of-track, the combination of a strong personality, a smattering of legal jargon plus common sense, a big impressive beard on an equally impressive man, and considerable skill with a six-shooter, all contributing to his authority. Racial clashes were always likely to erupt with so many Chinese and other foreigners as part of the work force, and things were often lively. 'Everything is perfectly peaceful here,' Bean told a visitor on one occasion. 'There hasn't been a man killed in four hours.'

The nearest court was some 200 miles away, so Bean's leaning towards the law was given growing scope. Soon the Texas Rangers brought in prisoners to his 'court', and on 2 August 1882, he was made a justice of the peace. At the Vinegaroon tent town he became famous for putting up the fines of those who dared answer him back, and with the backing of the Rangers his verdicts stuck.

Finally, with the tracks joined, and with a rival liquor dealer stealing much of his trade, Bean settled down at a spot he named Langtry in honour of the Jersey-born English actress, Lillie Langtry, known as the Jersey Lily. He is said to have fallen in love with her picture, so this actress mistress of the Prince of Wales (later Edward VII) became part of the legend of the West. Bean put THE JERSEY LILLY (sic) on his saloon courthouse, which is now a Texas shrine.

Bean's verdicts were liable to make legal history – of a sort. On one occasion he turned himself into a coroner as well as the judge. A railroad worker, who had fallen several hundred feet from a viaduct, was pronounced dead by Bean, who then decided that the five dollar coroner's fee was not big enough. So he switched himself from coroner to justice of the peace, examined the body, and found a pistol and $40. 'I find this corpse', he boomed gravely, 'guilty of carrying a concealed weapon, and I fine it $40!'

Few fines are known to have reached higher authorities. 'My court is self-sustaining' was his explanation, when challenged.

Perhaps his most famous – infamous by today's standards – ruling was in the case where a Chinese railroad worker had been killed in a brawl. A tough bunch of fellow-workers accompanied the accused, an Irishman, into court and Roy Bean was given to understand that the wrong ruling might be unfortunate for both his health and his business.

Bean examined his 'statoot' book, a blank book originally, which he had filled with such gems as 'Cheating and horse theft is hanging offenses if ketched'. On this occasion, however, he seemed in trouble, until he pointed firmly at a page, glared at all present, and intoned: 'Gents, this here court finds that the law is explicit on the killin' of a fellow man, but there ain't nothin' about knockin' off a heathen Chinee – case dismissed! And the drinks is on Paddy there!'

A very different and highly professional judge was Isaac 'Hanging Judge' Parker. Sensationalists have made him seem almost the equal of the infamous Judge Jefferies, who after the Battle of Sedgemoor in Somerset, England, in 1685, hanged, transported, whipped or fined hundreds of supporters of the rebel Duke of Monmouth during the 'Bloody Assize'. But in fact Judge Parker was in many ways an admirable man and was undeniably a good friend of the Indians for all his penchant for mass hangings.

Standards of Western justice were low, with too many lawyers totally unfitted for their jobs and a number of judges even less versed in their trade than Bean. And corruption was often gross. By these standards Parker was admirable, and when his judicial 'beat' is considered he was good by any standards. That beat was Indian Territory, now the state of Oklahoma.

In 1870, some 50,000 Indians were the official inhabitants of the area, the majority being the Five Civilised Tribes, late of the South – the Cherokees, Creeks, Choctaws, Chickasaws and Seminoles. The tribes had their own lands and were self-governing with American blessing, and they themselves were responsible for law and order. But already the territory was infested by white outlaws and other desperadoes, many of whom 'settled' there or used the huge area for hiding out between robberies.

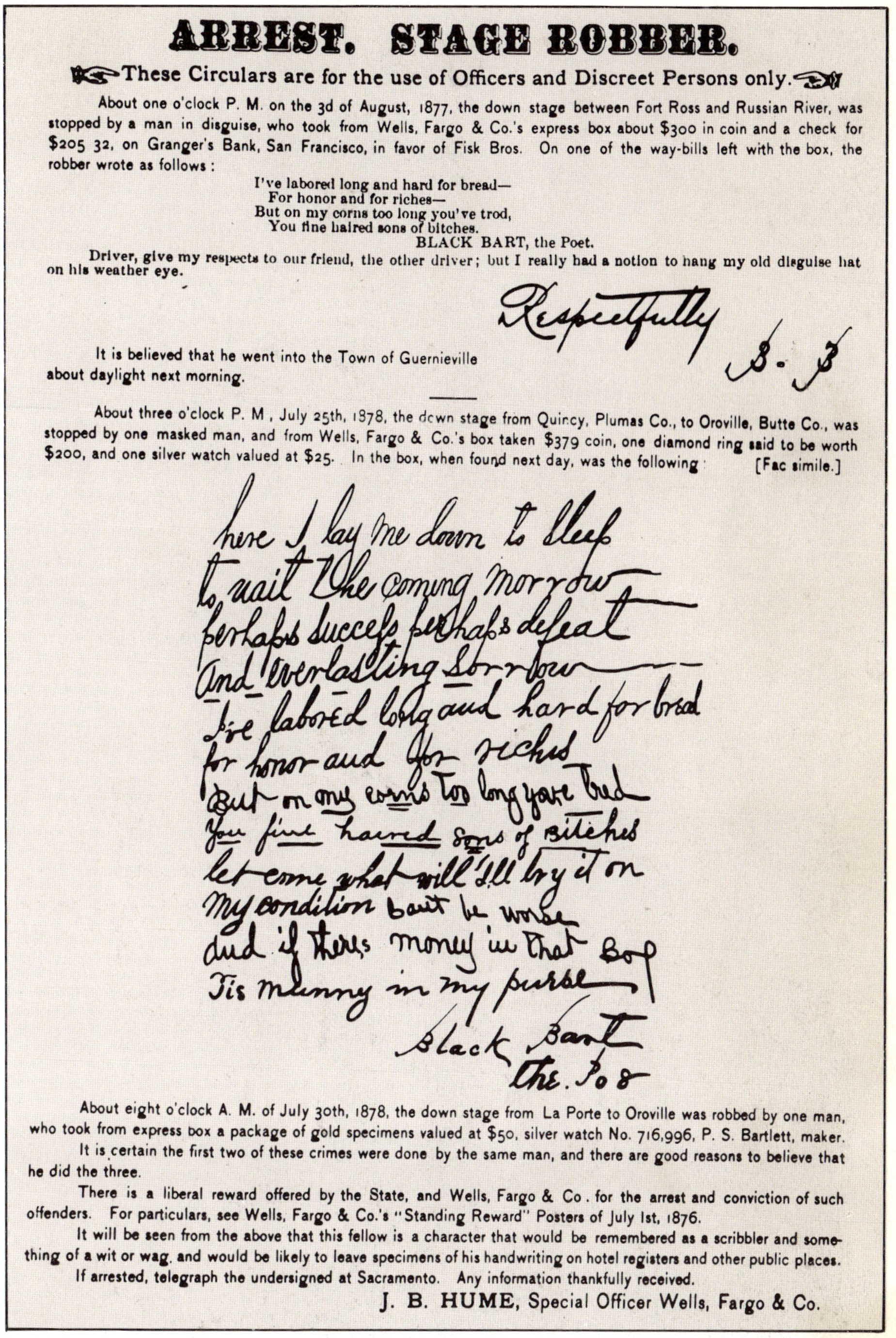

ARREST. STAGE ROBBER.

These Circulars are for the use of Officers and Discreet Persons only.

About one o'clock P. M. on the 3d of August, 1877, the down stage between Fort Ross and Russian River, was stopped by a man in disguise, who took from Wells, Fargo & Co.'s express box about $300 in coin and a check for $205 32, on Granger's Bank, San Francisco, in favor of Fisk Bros. On one of the way-bills left with the box, the robber wrote as follows:

I've labored long and hard for bread—
For honor and for riches—
But on my corns too long you've trod,
You fine haired sons of bitches.
BLACK BART, the Poet.

Driver, give my respects to our friend, the other driver; but I really had a notion to hang my old disguise hat on his weather eye.

Respectfully
B. B.

It is believed that he went into the Town of Guernieville about daylight next morning.

About three o'clock P. M, July 25th, 1878, the down stage from Quincy, Plumas Co., to Oroville, Butte Co., was stopped by one masked man, and from Wells, Fargo & Co.'s box taken $379 coin, one diamond ring said to be worth $200, and one silver watch valued at $25. In the box, when found next day, was the following: [Fac simile.]

here I lay me down to sleep
to wait the coming morrow
perhaps success perhaps defeat
And everlasting sorrow
I've labored long and hard for bread
for honor and for riches
But on my corns too long you've tred
You fine haired sons of Bitches
let come what will I'll try it on
My condition can't be worse
and if there's money in that Box
Tis munny in my purse
Black Bart
the Po8

About eight o'clock A. M. of July 30th, 1878, the down stage from La Porte to Oroville was robbed by one man, who took from express box a package of gold specimens valued at $50, silver watch No. 716,996, P. S. Bartlett, maker.

It is certain the first two of these crimes were done by the same man, and there are good reasons to believe that he did the three.

There is a liberal reward offered by the State, and Wells, Fargo & Co. for the arrest and conviction of such offenders. For particulars, see Wells, Fargo & Co.'s "Standing Reward" Posters of July 1st, 1876.

It will be seen from the above that this fellow is a character that would be remembered as a scribbler and something of a wit or wag, and would be likely to leave specimens of his handwriting on hotel registers and other public places.

If arrested, telegraph the undersigned at Sacramento. Any information thankfully received.

J. B. HUME, Special Officer Wells, Fargo & Co.

opposite
Charles E. Bolton (or Boles), alias 'Black Bart', who enjoyed robbing Wells Fargo coaches and leaving verses signed 'Black Bart the PO8'.

above
A famous poster quoting one of Black Bart's poems. James Hume finally tracked him down.

left
Bias against the Chinese could become lethal in the West.

below, left
Judge Roy Bean, whose methods and lack of legal training suggest the word judge should be put into quotes.

opposite
Judge Bean's courthouse, named 'The Jersey Lilly' in honour of Lillie Langtry, the Jersey-born actress whom he adored from afar.

More legitimately, cowboys crossed the territory, as we have seen, and railroad tracks spanned it, complete with depots. There were also stagecoach stations, so in the mid-1870s Indian Territory had a number of un-Indian place names on its map.

The five nations could not act judicially against whites of any sort, or even against their own people who joined white bands or committed crimes against whites. The law expected to administer this rogues' paradise was the US Court for the Western District of Arkansas, where a single judge and a small band of marshals were in charge of 70,000 square miles.

Naturally, the few legal white enterprises in the territory were followed by the usual enterprising Frontier riff-raff, plus many violent criminals. As the Arkansas lawmen were also responsible for much of their own state, precious little was done to help the unfortunate Indians, though in 1871, the judge, marshal and district attorney moved from Van Buren to Fort Smith, just 100 yards from Indian Territory. This step in the right direction was virtually nullified the following year when William Story, as useless as he was corrupt, was made federal judge. He was forced to resign less than two years later, his tenure of office having seen over 100 murders in the turbulent territory.

As if in answer to the Indians' prayers, a brilliant man actually volunteered to replace Story in 1875. It was Isaac Parker, then only thirty-six years old.

Parker was a devout Methodist and asked for the job when serving in Congress because he wanted to help the Indians – indeed, he pleaded their case so well that he was known as the 'Indians' best friend'. What could be better than the post at Fort Smith? With his wife and two children he left Missouri and headed for his destiny.

Parker was a fine figure of a man. His countenance bespoke Authority and such was his belief in his cause that the first sight of Fort Smith, which distressed his wife, made him even more determined to succeed.

He started off in robust style, trying ninety-one defendants in the eight weeks of his first session, eighteen being charged with murder and all but three being convicted. Six were condemned to death. 'I do not desire to hang you men. It is the law,' said Parker gravely, then he wept.

Five thousand people were present in the compound of the fort to see justice done upon a huge gallows, specially erected, and capable of sending a dozen men at a time into oblivion. There were children present plus clergy, and some hymn singing was heard: it was all much as that memorable movie, *True Grit*, was to portray it.

George Maledon was in charge, making sure that the six dropped simultaneously to a swift death. 'I never hanged a man who came back to have the job done over,' he later recalled with his gallows humour.

The mass hanging saw the start of a ground swell of hostility to Parker and his methods, especially in the East, but he got on with his job, having his marshal raise an army of 200 deputies. And Parker was given total power over the Territory, only the President being able to commute a death sentence by the 'Hanging Judge'.

Parker's army had few flawless men in it and plenty whom he rightly feared would be corrupt. He could not be too choosy, though he tried to select reasonably honest men – who got no salaries, simply fees and rewards for captures. He ordered them: 'Bring them in alive – or dead!' and sixty-five of his men were to die in the line of duty. This was war against outlawry in a single area on a scale never attempted before.

In fact, deputies did their best to bring men back alive, for there was an arrest fee on every man brought to trial, while a dead man, unless there was an alive-or-dead reward out for him, was worth nothing. They could, however, fine for small scale offences, or alleged ones, those who extorted money unjustly making a tough task even tougher, for soon the deputies were even less welcome with the less reprehensible denizens of the territory than they had been before.

But they were a success, so much so that congestion in the cells and courthouse was often total and the smells were appalling.

Parker was a quick worker who was in court six days a week, though he found time to make his mark

admirably in the day to day life of Fort Smith. He gave candy to children, enjoyed parties, never wore a gun, and had forty-six men hanged for murder and rape in his first fourteen years of office.

Gradually, his powers were lessened by Congress, first the size of his jurisdiction in the Territory, then, in 1889, with prisoners being allowed to appeal to the Supreme Court. But far more serious in a wider field was the opening up of 1.8 million acres of Indian land to white settlement in 1889, the first great land rush which drastically affected the Indians Parker had striven so hard to help. Naturally, the flood of whites produced a boom in outlawry, but Parker was ready for it, not least because he brought a brilliant lawman, Heck Thomas, to spearhead the attack on the new breed of outlaws.

Before dealing with them and the men who fought them, Judge Parker deserves a final salute. In March 1895, Indian Territory was no longer in his jurisdiction, a blow that, allied to attacks by young defence attorneys on his high-handed methods, and the Supreme Court's continual reversal of his decisions, finally broke his health. This was already crippled, unbeknown to any outside his family, by diabetes. He died in 1896 and at last the worth of the man was proclaimed. But the tributes that would have touched him most came from the Indians who knew his worth as few whites did. One of them, a Creek chief, brought wild flowers to his funeral.

The Oklahoma Guardsmen

Parker died on 17 November 1896, a few months after his lawmen had finally rid the Indian Territory of its most notable outlaw, Bill Doolin. It was Heck Thomas who finally got him, though he was one of a team of remarkable crimefighters working under US marshal Evett Nix. It was Nix who asked Judge Parker to bring in Heck Thomas, a Georgian-born Civil War veteran who had joined the Confederates at the age of twelve! After the war he made his name as a daring private detective, and when he reached Fort Smith he struck onlookers as a man who meant business in his knee-high boots and corduroy trousers, and armed with two six-shooters and an impressive-looking shotgun.

William 'Bill' Tilghman, late of the Dodge City police force where he was marshal in 1884, was another recruit, and a third splendid choice was Chris Madsen, Danish by birth, whose career was remarkable even by nineteenth-century standards. He had fought with the great Italian insurgent Garibaldi, joined the French Foreign Legion, then the US Cavalry, before becoming a lawman.

These three, under Nix's direction, were given areas in which to search for Doolin, the 'Oklahoma Guardsmen', as they were known, being independent but knowing what their colleagues were up to.

opposite
Isaac 'Hanging Judge' Parker did his best to protect the Indians of Indian Territory, later Oklahoma, even if his methods seemed extreme to Easterners who knew nothing of the situation there.

above
Temple Houston was the lawyer son of the great Texan, Sam Houston. He was a crack shot as well as a formidable orator in the court room.

Bill Doolin was a far more likeable outlaw than most, with brains, planning ability and a desire for money rather than excitement. His career might have ended in disaster with the Daltons at Coffeyville, but, luckily, as we have seen, he took no part in the raid. He and his gang flourished mightily as train and bank robbers with a good leader, dexterity with guns, and an excellent knowledge of Oklahoma Territory. They had a safe hideout in a cave on the Cimarron River and plenty of friends in the town of Ingalls, where Bill met the Methodist preacher's daughter who became his wife. His admirers quote his generosity, which was genuine, though they fail to mention where he got the money from. However, this ex-cowboy – a very skilled one – did actually give money to the poor, which makes a change.

It was Tilghman who accidentally discovered the hideout of the Doolin gang one bitter day in January 1895. Eight rifles were trained on him as he warmed himself at the fire, but he carefully failed to notice them, or their owners,

below
Bill Cook, alias John Williams, alias John Mayfield, an Oklahoma outlaw leader who finished up in prison.

right
Cherokee Bill had a good lawyer, who kept him alive for many months until Judge Parker finally got the killer to the gallows at Fort Smith.

opposite
Isom Dart, a Black cowboy (there were a number of them), who turned outlaw.

concealed in the bunks around the dugout. The sentimental version of the affair has Bill Doolin refusing to let his men shoot – 'Bill Tilghman's too good a man to be shot in the back'. But in *Bill Doolin, Outlaw O.T.* by Colonel Bailey C. Hanes, published as recently as 1968 by the University of Oklahoma Press, a more likely version is given, with Doolin and a henchman restraining a firebrand named Red Buck, Doolin telling him that by killing the popular marshal they would have a hundred men on them by the morning, complete with dynamite. In fact, Tilghman did return but the birds had flown.

Not until December 1895 did Tilghman finally catch up with Doolin, when the outlaw had gone to Eureka Springs, Arkansas, to treat his rheumatism in the waters. Tilghman, in a long coat and tall hat that made him look like a minister, entered the bathhouse in which Doolin was sitting reading a newspaper. The disguise fooled him.

Tilghman ordered a bath, then drew his pistol and pressed it against the outlaw's abdomen – or pointed it at him, from four feet away, depending on which account is accepted. He ordered him to put up his hands and surrender and Doolin slowly stood up, then, having protested his innocence, went for his shoulder holster. Tilghman at once jerked his wrist and said tensely: 'Bill, don't make me kill you!' Doolin sensibly surrendered and Tilghman sent off a short telegram to Nix – 'I have him. Will be home tomorrow.'

Later Bill Doolin was to say that he would never have let himself be taken if he had known Tilghman was on his own.

News of the capture of Bill Doolin swept Oklahoma and thousands thronged the station at Guthrie to see the 'outlaw who couldn't be captured' but had been. Marshal Nix rose to the occasion and had Doolin driven round Guthrie in a cab that sported Heck Thomas riding shotgun and other marshals inside. After his gala day Doolin was given a fine meal in the Royal Hotel, then planted firmly in jail. He had never been in prison before and he did not stay a captive long,

making a daring escape later that year, leading thirteen other prisoners to safety, including one of his gang known by the colourful nickname of 'Dynamite Dick'.

There seems little doubt that Bill Doolin had had enough of outlawry and that he planned to take his wife and young son away from the territory and settle down, perhaps in Mexico or Canada, or in New Mexico, where he had once told a friend he hoped to live in the San Andres Mountains. But Heck Thomas was tipped off as to where the family were hiding out – at a farmhouse in the Lawson area. He led a small posse there and noted the preparations for the move out of the territory, including a wagon.

Doolin was an ailing man and troubled by an old leg injury. It was common sense to clear out. And, with the posse stationed round the building, he came out, Winchester in hand, with his wife behind him, carrying their child. When he had helped them into the wagon, he started leading the horse away from the house. At that moment, Heck Thomas broke from the cover of bushes and shouted: 'Drop your gun and put up your hands!' Bill Doolin swung round, fired and missed, while Thomas aimed his shotgun and fired. Doolin fell dead.

Though the work of cleaning up Oklahoma was not yet complete, the death of the 'King of the Oklahoma Outlaws', as Bill Tilghman is said to have christened Doolin, was the beginning of the end. The spotlight was to switch northwards to Butch Cassidy and the Wild Bunch before the Wild West could be finally considered reasonably tame.

Bill Tilghman was to serve longer than any of the lawmen made famous in Oklahoma. He had arrived

$5,000.00

REWARD

FOR CAPTURE

DEAD OR ALIVE

OF

BILL DOOLIN

NOTORIOUS ROBBER OF TRAINS AND BANKS

ABOUT 6 FOOT 2 INCHES TALL, LT. BROWN HAIR, DANGEROUS, ALWAYS HEAVILY ARMED.

IMMEDIATELY CONTACT THE

U.S. MARSHAL'S OFFICE, GUTHRIE, OKLAHOMA TER.

opposite, above
A wooden jail in Wyoming Territory in 1893.

opposite, below
Bill Doolin was finally killed by Deputy U.S. Marshal Heck Thomas in 1896.

below
The jail at Clifton, Arizona, *c.* 1881.

there in 1889, becoming the first marshal of Perry, and he was to serve the territory and, later, the state for thirty-five years. He ranks high in the roster of Western peace officers as a professional and as a man, and he died with his boots on aged seventy in a wild oil town named Cromwell, whose marshal he had become against the advice of colleagues and friends. One night he heard a shot and made for the street, just as he might have done in Dodge City a generation earlier. He grabbed the man who had the gun, getting a bystander to take the weapon from him. But the man – ironically, a drunken prohibition officer – had a second gun which he drew and shot the great lawman, who died some minutes later. 'I want to go out in the smoke and die with my boots on,' he had said and he got his wish.

below
Fred McCarty and his father Bill were killed attempting to rob a bank at Delta, Colorado, in 1893.

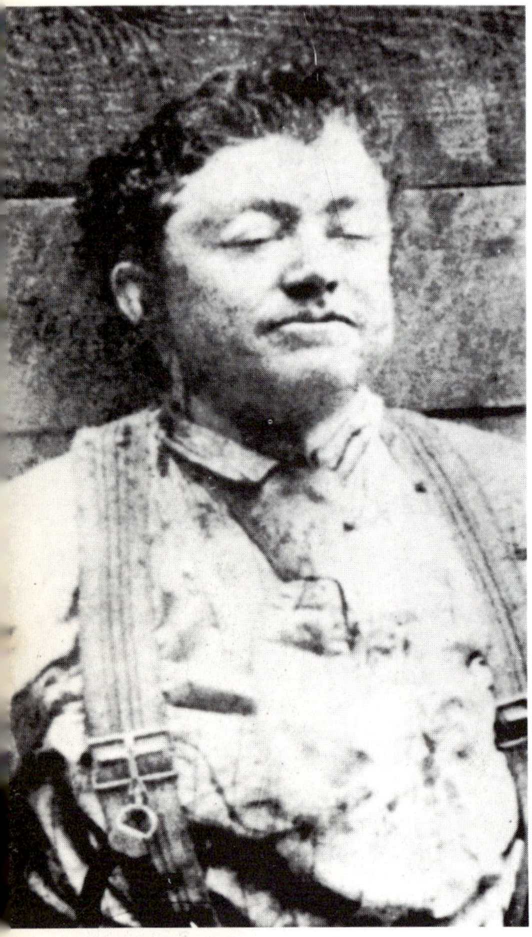

right
William 'Bill' Tilghman was one of the most notable Western lawmen, especially in Indian Territory in the 1890s.

Chapter 4

Range Wars

Of the many feuds that scarred the West, two stand out as Frontier epics, the Lincoln County War and the Johnson County War. No other episodes equalled them in high drama and memorable actors, though some 'wars' rivalled them in the atmosphere of sheer desperation which must have seized so many of the participants and innocent bystanders. And the feuding goes on long after the last participants have died. Arizona's Pleasant Valley War in the 1880s, which inspired Zane Gray's *To The Last Man* – an accurate title – was thought until 1977 to have been a cattlemen versus sheepmen confrontation with the half-Indian Tewksburys the villains and the Grahams the flawed heroes. Now, as this book is being written, new facts are coming from the Arizona Historical Society via a veteran historian, Clara T. Woody, which reverse parts of the accepted version of events as expounded in all sincerity by Earle R. Forrest in his thrilling *Arizona's Dark and Bloody Ground*. Happily, the sensational aftermath of the bloodbath

Two cowboys of the Hash Knife outfit, on the side of the Grahams in the Pleasant Valley War.

remains intact – how the young widow of the last of the Grahams went into court where his suspected killer, John Rhodes, was standing trial, how she drew her husband's six-shooter from her umbrella, pressed it into Rhodes' back and pulled the trigger.

It failed to go off, and, before the avenging widow could try again, uproar broke out in court and she was hustled away by her friends.

Few incidents that are authenticated in the Pleasant Valley War held such sensational drama as that, but the wars in Lincoln and Johnson counties were so dramatic that countless authors and screenplay writers have been blessing the participants ever since.

The first of them was the war in Lincoln County, New Mexico, and it was about power.

The Lincoln County War

Lincoln County, in the south-east of New Mexico, then consisted of a quarter of the territory, and it was the bloody struggle for economic and political power of the area that was rightly dubbed a war.

The population – what there was of it – was Mexican, American and Indian, indeed the wild land was not yet fully free from the Apache wars. Lincoln itself had once been a Mexican settlement and some miles away from it was Fort Stanton, built in 1855.

There is no shirking the seeds of this feud, for without them the resulting war cannot be fully understood. Two Civil War veterans, Laurence Murphy, an Irishman, and Emil Fritz, a German, started a store in Lincoln, which became known as the House. They were later joined by two younger Irishmen, James Dolan and John Riley.

Soon, they had much of the county 'sewn up', for they ran cattle on the ranges and also ran yet another Irishman, sheriff William Brady. Most lucrative of all were their contracts to supply the Mescalero Apaches on their reservation in the county with beef, and they also fed the troops at Fort Stanton. And to improve their position still further, they had useful cronies in the territorial capital, Santa Fe, an unattractive group of businessmen

left
John Tewksbury, who was killed in the Pleasant Valley War.

below
A Wyoming cowboy, ready for any emergency.

left
John Graham, one of the Graham clan, whose feud with the Tewksburys was amongst the deadliest on record. He was killed in 1887.

below
Edwin Tewksbury, half-Indian like his brother John, survived the Pleasant Valley War.

opposite
A striking drawing of vigilantes by Charles Russell.

and politicians known as the Santa Fe Ring, just the sort of unscrupulous gang for men on the make to know.

The war broke out in 1878, by which time Murphy was in virtual retirement from illness and Fritz was dead. This gave Riley and, especially, the even more ruthless Dolan, their chance.

The House was loathed and also feared by most of the small-time ranchers and settlers of the county. They were made to take low prices for their cattle, forced to buy goods at inflated prices and, worse, feel insecure in their properties. As for the partners in the House, they managed to stay on excellent terms with the senior officers at the fort – Dolan and Riley were both really first-rate conmen – and were able to see to it that the Apaches were swindled out of their official rations. And to add to the general misery in the county, lawlessness was rife, cattle rustling being rampant and death commonplace.

Suddenly, the Murphy mafia found it had rivals, a trio who were unblushingly ambitious, by no means lacking in ruthlessness, but compared with their grossly corrupt and essentially evil opponents, basically reputable and certainly infinitely more likeable.

The most powerful of them was cattle king John Chisum, the shrewd but benevolent ruler of a mighty slice of ranchland along the Pecos River. He was eager to take over the House's beef contracts and had good ground for assuming that Murphy men were stealing his stock.

Chisum befriended an able young Scots–Canadian lawyer named Alexander McSween, who came with his wife from a law office in Kansas. Like John Chisum (who, of course, was too important to need to), McSween never carried a gun.

The third man was English. He was John Tunstall, who arrived in 1876. He was the son of a wealthy London merchant and had come to New Mexico via Canada and California, and now, partnered by McSween, and helped by his father's and Chisum's money, he opened a store/bank just a quarter of a mile from the House. McSween had

political hopes, but Tunstall was strictly a businessman, writing to his father that he intended to control the county and take 50 cents of every dollar spent there. Such designs were a certain invitation to gunsmoke.

The new store was popular with most local people because it was honest and because it was not the House, whose owners saw trade vanishing from them. Tempers were not improved because McSween had fallen out with the House over Fritz's will. He had been employed as the only lawyer on the spot, but now false accusations were being thrown at him. With the local press carrying charge and countercharge, and with McSween refusing to give urgently needed insurance money to Dolan and Riley, tension mounted. Dolan succeeded in having McSween arrested for alleged embezzlement and even had Chisum arrested for a spell for alleged debts.

Power lay in the hands of the House, for the trio had only the small-timers of the county to back them and – fortunately – some tough young cowhands. John Tunstall's foreman – the Englishman was rancher as well as storekeeper – was a handsome young man with a small ranch of his own, Dick Brewer, and one of the men under him was Billy the Kid. His story belongs to the next chapter, but he was to play a notable part in the war that was so soon to erupt. Tunstall had taken a liking to the youth who had arrived with a cloud hanging over him, small as that cloud was, whatever legends suggest.

The House might be short of cash, but its overall power was still intact and backed up by plenty of rustlers and killers on their payroll.

Sheriff Brady was now put to work by his bosses. He followed up a writ of attachment on McSween's property with an even more improper one on everything in Tunstall's store.

There followed the tragedy that started the war. On 18 February 1878, John Tunstall left his ranch for Lincoln, driving six horses that Brady had agreed could be excluded from the writ of attachment. Neither he nor McSween fully appreciated the extreme danger of their situation or the ruthlessness of their opponents, but at least Tunstall had some tough Westerners to ride with him that day: Dick Brewer, Billy the Kid, John Middleton and Robert Widenmann. They could not know that a far bigger posse was gunning for them, well stocked with criminals and led by sheriff Brady's deputy, Mathews.

Brewer and Widenmann had ridden ahead hoping to spot wild turkeys, when they looked back and saw some men riding towards Tunstall. The rest of the posse was some way behind them.

The two men shouted at the other three and Middleton and the Kid galloped to them under the impression that Tunstall was with them. Bullets sped them on their way and they took cover.

Meanwhile, their employer had turned to await the riders. He could not be seen by his men because of some trees, out of which three of the posse appeared. They were William Morton, Jessie (sic) Evans, recently escaped from jail and with a reputation for viciousness, and Tom Hill, an equally unlikely choice for a legal posse.

It is assumed that Morton shot Tunstall out of his saddle. Then Evans took the dead man's gun and fired into his body. He was shooting Tunstall's horse when the rest of the posse reached the spot. Morton told them that the Englishman had fired first, the unfortunate Englishman who imagined that fair play existed in Lincoln County.

Behind their sheltering boulders, the four Tunstall men knew what must have happened. With Western common sense they had not tried to rescue their boss, which would have been suicidal. They hastened to Lincoln, the killers and their cronies following them and bandying it about that Tunstall had been shot resisting arrest.

Tunstall senior later filed claims for compensation and documents sailed to and fro across the Atlantic, the claim finally being refuted in 1885. By then the distraught father had been dead three years.

Dick Brewer and the other Tunstall men wanted revenge, indeed Billy the Kid is alleged to have

above
Frederic Remington drew this graphic picture of a dispute over a brand.

opposite
Cattle baron John Chisum was in partnership with Tunstall and McSween but he managed to avoid taking direct action in the Lincoln County War.

sworn an oath over his ex-employer's grave: 'Tunstall was the only man that ever treated me decent. I'll kill the men who did this to him!'

Revenge on the probable killer came swiftly. At the head of eleven 'Regulators', who were holding warrants supplied by an anti-House J.P., Brewer captured William Morton and Frank Baker, another of the posse. There is no doubt that Brewer wanted to bring back his prisoners alive but that Billy the Kid and others wanted to exact instant revenge. The events that followed remain confused, but the results are not: Morton and Baker were killed, the former, it is said, with nine bullet holes in his back; one of the Regulators, William McCloskey, also died, either because he had sworn to protect the prisoners (the Dolan version) or because Morton, riding with him, had managed to grab his gun and kill him (the less likely Tunstall-McSween supporters' version).

By now the atmosphere in and around Lincoln was extremely tense. Dolan's men looked forward to the future – 'Tunstall is gone. We must get McSween next' – while Dolan himself without much difficulty made sure that the governor saw things the House way, a way that included removing the deputy US marshalship of Robert Widenmann, who as one of Tunstall's men had been stirring up trouble in his official capacity. First and second rounds to the House . . .

Yet it was McSween's supporters who went into violent action first, ambushing sheriff Brady and his deputies, Mathews, Peppin and Hindman. The gunmen were behind a wall by Tunstall's store and they killed Brady and mortally wounded Hindman. Billy the Kid was slightly wounded when picking up a Winchester beside Brady, which the sheriff had confiscated from him some time before.

As for the other two present at the killing of Tunstall, after their posse duty they returned to their old ways and Hill was killed trying to rob a sheepherder's camp. Evans was wounded in the wrist and the lung, but lived to fight another day.

The next battle was an epic. It happened on 4 April 1878, less than two months after Tunstall's death, when Dick Brewer and a dozen other Regulators ambushed and finally killed Andrew 'Buckshot' Roberts, who fought like a superman before going down fighting, taking Brewer with him. For sheer guts and determination his last stand at Blazer's Mill was rarely equalled in the whole history of the West.

The origins of 'Buckshot' or 'Buckshot Bill' Roberts are obscured by too many contradictory stories, noted in the finest account of him in *The Gunfight at Blazer's Mill* by Colin Rickards in a monograph published by the University of Texas Press in 1974. It seems certain that Roberts was a Southerner who went to New Mexico around 1875 and began ranching in a small way. Old-timers recalled him as a shabby little man, his nickname coming from a buckshot wound in his right shoulder, though no-one could later say how and when he received it. He could not raise his rifle so gamely shot from the hip.

Blazer's Mill was named for its owner, Dr Joseph Blazer, and it was on the Mescalero Apache Reservation. Blazer, an ex-dentist, was now in the timber business and, when the Indian Agency was set up, his property, which was very efficiently run, remained in his hands and much of the Agency's affairs were conducted there.

Roberts used to visit a friend named Sam Miller who worked at Blazer's Mill. There was no reason for him to have joined the posse that killed Tunstall, though, possibly, he needed the fee. He was certainly not immediately implicated in the killing, and his friend Miller recalled how he had stoutly maintained that he was not even with the posse, but with a group of those who were left behind at Tunstall's ranch.

That was no concern of the Regulators. They were after anyone connected, even remotely, with the slaying, and Roberts decided it was high time he left Lincoln County. He sold his spread and arranged that a cheque for it should be sent to the post office run by Blazer.

Though not backed by contemporary records, there is a local tradition that Roberts had an extra reason for waiting anxiously for his money, for the story goes that Billy the Kid and another Regulator, Charlie Bowdre, ran into Roberts in late March and, presumably thinking they were out to get him, he fired on them from a distance. They recognised him as they rode away unharmed. His detractors, however, have claimed that he had become a bounty hunter, as rewards were out for those who had killed Brady and Hindman. As he was eagerly scanning each delivery of mail now, this hardly seems likely.

He was waiting for the mail carrier on 4 April at the settlement's main building, a twin-storied house originally fortified against Indian attacks, now used as a trading post, restaurant and lodging house as well as for Agency business. The mill was about 250 yards from the multi-purpose building.

When an Apache herder reported that a band of men had killed a steer the previous night, Blazer, having little doubt as to who they were, appealed to Roberts to leave at once, not wanting the lives of women and children risked in a gun-battle. Roberts agreed to go after asking that his money be sent on elsewhere by Dr Blazer, then he swiftly loaded his belongings onto his pack-horse, mounted his mule, and soon left the main road, taking to a trail through timber to avoid running into the Regulators.

His pursuers arrived at the Mill and, after leaving their horses in a corral, went inside to eat. Roberts sealed his fate the moment he spotted the mail carrier, for not knowing that the Regulators were at Blazer's Mill, he turned and rode back there. The corral was too high for him to spot the horses and, obeying Blazer's standing rule about 'parking' weapons, left his gun belt on his saddle horn and walked towards the door on the building's west side.

below
Alexander McSween, the Canadian-born lawyer and friend of John Tunstall. Like Tunstall, he was killed in the Lincoln County War.

above, right
Mrs McSween, a heroic and tragic figure in the Lincoln County War, who stood up to the men who killed her husband.

opposite
John Tunstall, the Englishman whose murder triggered off the Lincoln County War.

The best account of what happened next has come down to us from Frank Coe, one of the Regulators, who knew Roberts and almost fifty years later gave an account that, with due allowance made for lapses of memory, is thought to be accurate. His cousin George and other witnesses also left their own versions.

John Middleton, who guarded the horses while his companions had a meal, saw 'a mighty-well-armed' man hitching his mule outside and reported the fact to Dick Brewer. In Lincoln County that was hardly enough to leave one's meal for and the others took little notice. Frank Coe happened to finish first, went outside, and on seeing his friend, shook him by the hand and sat down in a side door with him. He urged him forcibly to surrender – by his own account for nearly half an hour.

Meanwhile, the other Regulators, having finished eating, had started appearing, Dick Brewer being forced, not for the first time, to restrain his more explosive-tempered men. Coe and Roberts went on talking, then around the corner came Charlie Bowdre, Frank MacNab, John Middleton, George Coe, and Henry Newton Brown; Brown, as we have seen, was to become marshal of

Caldwell, then lead a disastrous bank raid on Medicine Lodge.

'Buckshot' Roberts got up and faced his enemies at some fifteen feet.

Bowdre spoke first. 'Throw up your hands or you are a dead man!'

'Not much, Mary Ann,' Roberts retorted, bringing his rifle up to his hip. Bowdre was already pointing his pistol and both men fired simultaneously. Bowdre's shot 'struck Roberts right through the middle', said George Coe, while Roberts' bullet had an extraordinary career, shooting off Bowdre's gun-belt, which fell on the ground, then ricochetting and mangling George Coe's trigger thumb and finger, forcing his pistol from his hand as he fired. Along with Bowdre, he ducked for cover.

That should have been the end of the matter as the Regulators opened up on Roberts, but, incredibly, he was not hit and, as he retreated along the wall, he managed to send a bullet searing into John Middleton's lung.

His carbine was now empty, and Billy the Kid, realising this, ran towards Roberts to finish the battle off. The tough old-timer had other ideas, using his carbine as a bayonet and winding him painfully, causing the Kid to miss, though that was not what he told his friends when he got back to them.

Meanwhile, Roberts had made Dr Blazer's office, leaning in what must have been agony against the wall. With no ammunition and with his pistol on his mule, he needed luck and had it, for he saw Blazer's Springfield 45–60 in the room, where there was also plenty of ammunition. He dragged a matress from a cot and put it in front of the partly opened door, then he got down, loaded and started firing.

At a council of war, the Regulators debated whether to rush Roberts or let him die. But suddenly Roberts found an ally, a scout and trader who worked for the Agency called Numa Strain, who began working his way to his friend. Roberts saw him but urged him away – and so did a threatening Billy the Kid. He retreated, hoping to summon volunteers to Roberts' aid, but there were none.

The Kid told Dr Blazer to order Roberts out, at which the doctor pointed out that Roberts was just as likely to shoot him as anyone else.

With the day getting steadily hotter, and with F. C. Godfroy, the Indian agent, tending the wounded – George Coe, Bowdre and Middleton – Dick Brewer impatiently ordered Blazer to bring Roberts out and said he would burn the house down otherwise. The doctor still refused, so a furious Brewer began creeping to a spot near the saw mill, where he took up a position behind some logs. One other man, possibly Bowdre, was with him. Then Brewer carefully aimed at the doorway and fired. There was silence.

Concluding that 'Buckshot' was dead or out of action, the handsome leader of the Regulators raised himself up for another shot, and took a bullet from Roberts in the middle of his forehead which, as Frank Coe recalled it, tore off the top of his head.

Even before this stupendous – or lucky – piece of marksmanship, the other Regulators had decided to pull

out and get their wounded medical help, and now, with their leader killed, they headed for Frank Coe's ranch.

Back at the scene of the action, Dr Blazer found it hard going to make Roberts believe that his enemies had left, not least because the dying hero was becoming trigger happy and liable to shoot at anything that moved. It needed a white cloth carried by an old man to get Roberts into a peaceable frame of mind, and soon the doctor and the agent's family were making him as comfortable as possible. Brewer was buried fast because of the strong sun, and the next day the valiant cripple was buried beside him.

The war went on, reaching a climax in the notorious five-day pitched battle in Lincoln itself, which claimed a notable victim in McSween. The battle began on 14 July, when up to fifty of his supporters rode in to recapture the town, which by then was in the hands of the Dolan faction. The invaders' timing was good, for most of sheriff George 'Dad' Peppin's men were away keeping watch on another area, and he was taken by surprise.

The McSween men firmly established themselves in three buildings, barricading windows, piling dirt-filled sandbags against doors and drilling portholes through walls to such good effect that it made them impregnable enough to sustain a longish siege. Their top men, Americans and Mexicans, were with McSween in his own home, as was his remarkable wife Susan, determined to stay with her husband. And meanwhile, Peppin's absent men returned to Lincoln and made themselves as impregnable as the opposition.

So secure was each side that the first three days of the 'battle' were mainly notable for the expenditure of ammunition and the deaths of a horse and a mule. On the human side, one of Peppin's men was seriously wounded. What turned the battle from stalemate to a victory for the Dolans was the intervention of the military.

Dolan had been hoping for this, that Colonel Dudley at Fort Stanton would opt for the law and order party, as he foolishly believed it to be. Because of new army regulations he could not move soldiers into town yet, so Dolan, cunning and persuasive for all his blustering and hot-headedness, went to Dudley to get him to change his mind.

Dudley had always favoured the House and now he was in Dolan's pocket, not because he was a rogue like the Irishman, but because he was prejudiced and a fool. He elected to send troops to Lincoln 'for the preservation of the lives of women and children, and in response to numerous petitions received from persons in that town'.

So it came about that the McSween supporters on 19 July found themselves facing a Gatling gun, a mountain howitzer, and a contingent, including thirty men and every officer from Fort Stanton save Lieutenant Pogue, left to command the fort. They had rations for three days. The military were supposed to be neutral, a laughable supposition in view of the way things actually turned out.

Colonel Dudley soon showed his hand by signing a warrant made out against McSween, while by this time the appearance of the troops so frightened the biggest bunch of McSween men that they fled from their posts at the Montano House. Though the majority were Mexicans, three of them were experienced Tunstall-McSween fighters, Middleton, Bowdre and 'Doc' Scurlock, all of them hard-core Regulators.

The situation of the McSween men deteriorated rapidly. The lawyer did his best to challenge Dudley's actions, without any success, and it appears that he was prepared to surrender – to Dudley, not to Peppin and his unsavoury gang.

Peppin's men set fire to McSween's house and his wife left to plead her husband's cause with Colonel Dudley. She had crawled on her hands and knees to reach her front door, but outside she was safe from bullets. She asked the colonel, who protested his neutrality, why therefore was a cannon pointed at her house? Dudley laughed at her and suggested it was in fact pointing the other way, and soon he was claiming that he had no idea that it was Peppin's men who had fired her house. After more futile exchanges with the blinkered commander, she returned to the burning building. In the light of later events, it was by no means certain that the Frontier rule not to harm women would be obeyed, for her brave speaking enflamed the Dolan faction.

In the McSween house a conference was called, with Billy the Kid for the first time coming forward as leader: McSween had sunk to depths of depression that made him incapable of caring what happened. Billy suggested a run for the river, asking Mrs McSween to go before the men – 'a dress ain't very good to make a run in' – and very reluctantly she said she would.

Later, when the flames had virtually gutted the house except for a single room, Billy and two others made the first break for safety. He and another made the river, but one Harvey Morris died. So did McSween, who with the rest delayed their escape longer than Billy had said they should. They tried to surrender, but no-one was interested, and five were shot down, McSween being – as usual – unarmed. Later Susan McSween was to recall how her husband fell on his knees and cried: 'I surrender. Oh, my God save me! Oh, Lord, Lord save me!' Instead they shot him like a cur, then broke up burning boards and flung them onto his lifeless body. His courage had remained unshaken earlier in the war, but at the last the will to live seemed to leave him – and with his death the war ended. A judge later vindicated him and summed up the participants accurately: 'Both sides have done many things contrary to law. McSween I firmly believe acted conscientiously; Murphy and Co, for private gain and revenge.' Few who have studied the war since have disagreed with that verdict.

Subsequently, Billy the Kid really became a criminal, as we shall see in the next chapter. Alas, the leading villain, James Dolan, though he lost J. J. Dolan and Co. by mortgage foreclosure, later prospered

This picture is usually printed in reverse – hence the legend of Billy the Kid, the 'left-handed gun'. Here it is correctly printed.

mightily. He successfully entered New Mexico politics and Tunstall's properties came his way. Finally, he died rich in 1898. He had been just thirty years old when the five-day battle of Lincoln raged.

John Chisum had not taken an active part in the war, though, as we shall see in the next chapter, he and Billy the Kid were to have an interesting confrontation. As for Susan McSween, we left her at the point of her husband's death. Two days later she was searching the ruins of her home when a Dolan man, Andy Boyle, began laughing at her attempts to rescue a partly burned carpet of some value. 'By God,' chortled the gross Boyle, 'we've killed McSween and we'll get you next!'

'Well, kill me,' rejoined this extraordinary woman. 'You have already taken away all that was precious to me, my husband and my home. I'd just as soon you'd take my life.'

A companion of Boyle's, John Kinney, threatened to take her at her word, but her courage must have shamed the appalling pair and they left her in peace. It is said that John Chisum gave her a small herd of cattle, and she did indeed become a successful rancher, living on until 1931. As for what happened in the months after the war proper ended, it belongs to the story of Billy the Kid.

The Johnson County War

The Johnson County War was also a struggle for power, but this time cattle were at the heart of the matter, not on the fringes. Again, the war has been a gift to authors of books and screenplays, and again there was an episode of heroism by a single man, this time of Homeric proportions. Even the hero's name was right, for he was on the side of the ordinary people of Johnson County. His name – Champion.

So stirred were the feelings of these people, the small ranchers and settlers, and their opponents, the cattle barons and their henchmen, that a ferocious polemic by the writer and publisher, A. S. Mercer, *The Banditti of the Plains,* which appeared at the time, became virtually unobtainable. Even the copyright copies in the Library of Congress got 'lost', and its enemies were so eager to suppress the book and so hostile to its author that he was

opposite, above
The Cheyenne Club, headquarters of Wyoming's cattle barons.

opposite, below
Stick 'em up: a drawing by Charles Russell.

below
Ella Watson was a harmless enough whore who may have taken some stolen cattle in exchange for her favours.

lucky to leave Wyoming alive. Fortunately, the University of Oklahoma republished Mercer's book in 1954 when things had started to calm down a little. The subtitle is a strong one – 'The Cattlemen's Invasion of Wyoming in 1892', but this was too tame for Mercer, who added another in brackets: (THE CROWNING INFAMY OF THE AGES). Strong language, but, as in the Lincoln County War, passions and fears ran at volcanic pitch and exaggeration was pardonable.

The seeds of the conflict were laid in the 1870s and '80s. What became Johnson County had seen plenty of action in the 1860s, when the Bozeman Trail ran through it to the goldfields of Montana and caused Red Cloud's War (1866–68), the war the Indians won, for it ended with the troops withdrawing from Fort Phil Kearny and leaving it to the Indians to burn. But, of course, the white man won in the end and the Powder River country, though it saw more Indian fighting in the '70s, gradually became a cattleman's paradise.

Many of Wyoming's early ranchers made fortunes on the open ranges, some of them becoming cattle barons. There seems little doubt that some helped themselves advance faster by rustling and branding strays, but were quite prepared to condemn their enemies later for the same crimes. And down the years 'sodbusters' and small ranchers – or men who combined both farming and a modest amount of cattle raising – came to the territory. The Homestead Act of 1862 had offered free land – 160 acres – to anyone who wanted it and the land in Wyoming was good.

In the mid-1880s the range suffered a series of calamities. There was overstocking and drought and the price of beef fell steeply in 1886, and that winter, the worst in recorded Western history, wiped out about three-quarters of Wyoming's cattle.

In fact, those ranchers who came through the disaster learnt from their mistakes. They grew hay for the winter and introduced new stock. The longhorns gave way to cross-breeds or high-class breeds from Britain and the ranchers saw to it that the range would never be overstocked again. Ranching was becoming scientific. By now barbed wire was spreading over the West and was causing much bloodshed, as it spelled doom to the old open range, but there was plenty of that left in Wyoming – and a steady stream of settlers 'squatting' on it. When the territory became a state in 1890 the situation was approaching explosion point.

The cattle barons had begun to think of all these 'intruders' on to their domain as rustlers and it would be foolish to deny that some of them were. Yet most were ordinary folk working hard to make a living.

It must be stressed that the cattle barons, talking the situation over in the plush Cheyenne Club (which was like a London or New York gentlemen's club, transported West), were not a bunch of villains like the House and the Santa Fe Ring in New Mexico. But they became corrupt and villainous when they saw their futures threatened. They had real power. The Wyoming Stock Growers' Association, which mustered around a hundred members, included the state governor and its senators, which certainly smoothed things for the other members. An extraordinary 'maverick law' was introduced, which gave the right to a rancher to claim any unbranded calf found wandering on the range. The law was said to be aimed at rustlers, but its immoral aftermath was the system by which strays were auctioned at prices that were normally too high for the unfortunate small cattlemen to reclaim them.

The vicious circle continued because the money made by the auctions paid the wages of detectives hired by the big ranchers – and if any of these detectives secured a conviction of a rustler he got a splendid $250.

The Association hired as their chief detective a ruthless gunfighter, Frank Canton, who had been sheriff of Johnson County. He had earlier been a bank robber, rustler and killer, though the citizens of Wyoming did not know this as he had changed his name (previously Horner). The people of Johnson County were by no means pleased to find that Canton – who was later to be one of Judge Parker's deputies in Oklahoma – had been bought up by the opposition, and events were to prove them right.

The worst proof came outside Johnson County on the Sweetwater Range to the south. There, beside the river, were two settlers: Jim Averill, who ran a small store which included a saloon and a post office, and Ella Watson, a Canadian-born whore from Kansas, who sometimes received payment in cattle, not money, from her cowboy patrons. Alas, they lived on land that was used for grazing and 'owned' by a boorish, boastful rancher named Albert Bothwell. Averill chose this moment to write in the Casper *Weekly Mail* in April 1889 that the cattle barons were land grabbers and speculators, which, coming from a justice of the peace, was strong talk. In July, he paid for his boldness, for Bothwell and some of his cronies arrived at the cabins where Averill and Ella lived and, without even mounting the semblance of a trial, strung them both up beside each other on a nearby tree. When the inevitable outcry occurred, suitable propaganda turned poor Ella into the notorious rustler queen 'Cattle Kate', a mythical creation that actually made the front of the *Police Gazette*, and who was said to have had to die 'for the good of the county'. Naturally, no-one was ever prosecuted for the double lynching. It was a bestial business.

opposite
Propaganda turned poor Ella Watson into 'Cattle Kate', a rustler queen. Here she is being strung up with her friend, James Averill.

above
James Averill, hanged alongside Ella Watson, dared to stand up to cattle baron Albert Bothwell and was 'executed' for his pains.

Next to be 'executed' was a horse-raiser named Waggoner, who was summoned from his home by three men with false papers and found eight days later hanging from a tree some miles away in a spot which became known as 'Dead Man's Canyon'.

The lynching occurred in June 1891, but the next act in the drama was less successful from the point of view of the members of the Cheyenne Club. Would-be assassins appeared at the cabin of W. H. Hall on the Powder River. The owner was away, but his roommates, Ross Gilberston and Nathan D. Champion, were inside on their bunks. Two of the intruders remained outside while the other two broke in, one of them shouting: 'Give up, we have got you this time.' Then he fired at Champion and missed.

Nate Champion, a Texan of Alamo quality, seized his gun and started firing to such effect that he put all four to flight, two of them being wounded.

These two left their overcoats behind, so it was easy to identify them. Yet only one was arrested; he was bailed for a large sum and left the state.

The next two killings raised the temperature in Johnson County to boiling point, for the men, Orley Jones and John Tisdale, both had fine reputations and had never been accused of cattle rustling. Jones, who was soon to be married, was callously murdered by an assassin lurking under a bridge, while poor Tisdale's corpse was found in his wagon. He had been bringing home Christmas toys to his children and they lay around him, stained in blood. Frank Canton's horse was found near the spot. Tisdale had told friends in Buffalo that he had heard Canton tell someone that he would take care of Tisdale, and had feared for his life, buying a double-barrelled shotgun for the journey. It did him little good against an experienced killer. Canton was arrested, but after a preliminary hearing of two days he was released. Most people were convinced there had been corruption.

The small ranchers and settlers organised themselves in the Northern Wyoming Farmers' and Stock Growers' Association, while their enemies plotted their extinction. One of them on a visit to Denver, Colorado, stated that nine-tenths of the people of Wyoming sympathised with the cattle owners and said: 'I am willing to give all the assistance possible to any body of men which will attempt to exterminate the rustlers.'

A death list of seventy names was drawn up and a recruiting drive was launched to find suitable killers. Kentucky-born Major Frank Wolcott, now a cattleman and once an army officer, had been suggesting an invasion of Johnson County for some time and now the portly veteran got his chance. The immoral plan that was drawn up was a good one: raise the force from outside Wyoming, cut all the telegraph lines linking the county to the rest of the state, then make for Buffalo, the county seat and a hotbed of 'nesters', rustlers and their supporters, so it was claimed. There, it was vital to kill sheriff 'Red' Angus, his deputies and the local commissioners, all of whom were on the side of 'evil', then the invaders would lethally deal with the death list.

There was no need to keep the great plan secret from anyone in authority. Dr Amos Barber, the Acting Governor of Wyoming, knew about it and gave the expedition a brand-new case of guns. The state senators knew about it, too, while the National Guard was ordered to disregard all orders unless they came from state headquarters, a

opposite
The mounted man on the left is Nate Champion, the supreme hero of the Johnson County War, in which he made an epic last stand against more than fifty men.

left
The traditional penalty for alleged and actual cattle rustlers.

below
Major Frank Wolcott, the pompous leader of the Johnson County invaders.

flat violation of state laws, for local authorities were allowed to call them out in any emergency. As for the officials of Union Pacific, they laid on a special train to bring the invaders into the state.

Meanwhile, horses were obtained from Colorado in case too big a roundup in Wyoming might alert the enemy, and Tom Smith, not to be confused with the heroic marshal of Abilene featured in the previous chapter, but a detective of the W.S.G.A., left for Texas with a recruiting party offering excellent terms: $5 a day and expenses, and a bonus for each man for every 'rustler' killed. Each volunteer was insured for $3,000.

On 6 April 1892, a Pullman reached Casper, Wyoming, and from it emerged fifty-two men, most of them heavily armed, twenty-two being mercenaries from Texas. The ride had been eventful. The gunfighters had travelled separately from their employers, the Wyoming cattlemen, not that the Texans seem to have been anxious to mix with them. But a moment of tension came when Frank Canton entered the stockmen's private car to be ordered out by the pompous Wolcott. An ill-timed quarrel culminated in Wolcott resigning, Tom Smith taking charge of the Texans and Canton of the whole expedition, though, as things turned out, Wolcott regained control later when Canton's powers of leadership proved inadequate.

There were two reporters along with the invaders, Sam Clover of the *Chicago Herald*, and Ed Towse of the *Cheyenne Sun*, both of whom were guaranteed to give the right slant to their readers. And now it was time to advance: the wires had been cut, a horse had finally been found for the party's heavyweight, Jim Dudley. The ordinary people of Johnson County were totally isolated.

The invaders headed for a ranch owned by a member of the W.S.G.A., confusingly called, like one of its victims, John Tisdale. They were now poised to enter Johnson County. But instead of pressing on directly to Buffalo, that haunt of alleged rustlers, the expedition headed for another alleged band at the KC Ranch, reaching it on 9 April soon after daybreak. It was a bitterly cold morning with snow flurries in the wind, and the gang within the hut consisted of the valiant Nate Champion, who, as we have seen, had already driven off one small band of assassins, and his friend Nick Ray. Both featured on the death list despite the fact that there was no evidence that either were rustlers. Also with the pair were two trappers who had sheltered overnight from the storm with them.

The cabin was soon surrounded and out of it came the trappers, to be rounded up and sent away. Ray came out to find where they had got to and the invaders opened fire, mortally wounding him. He began to crawl back when Nate came out, grabbed his collar and pulled him to safety. He used one hand, firing his six-shooter with the other.

And now began an epic so magnificent that even professional debunkers, sitting comfortably in their air-conditioned rooms, have never managed to touch it. Nate Champion, a Texan, like so many of those who sought to kill him, kept up a day-long battle and, astonishingly, and fortunately for posterity, managed to leave the people of Johnson County an account of his struggle. He wrote it in a pocket book that was later found soaked in his blood and with a bullet hole through it. Here are some excerpts from it:

Me and Nick was getting breakfast when the attack took place. Two men was with us – Bill Jones and another man. The old man went out for water and did not come back. His friend went to see what was the matter and he did not come back. Nick started out and I told him to look out, that I thought there was someone at the stable and would not let them come back. Nick is shot but not dead yet. He is awful sick. I must go and wait on him. It is now about two hours since the first shot. Nick is still alive; they are still shooting and are all around the house. Boys, there is bullets coming in like hail. Them fellows is in such shape I can't get at them. They are shooting from the stable and river and back of the house. Nick is dead.

The endless day dragged on. Later he wrote that he thought they had fired the stable. 'I don't think they intend me to get away this time,' he went on, and confessed that he felt pretty lonesome and wished he had someone else with him so that they could watch all sides at once. The besiegers finally decided to burn him out and pushed a wagonload of hay up to his cabin, then lit it. The diary ended thus:

below
Sheriff 'Red' Angus, on the side of the small ranchers and homesteaders in the Johnson County War.

Well, they have just got through shelling the house like hell. I heard them splitting wood. I guess they are going to fire the house tonight. I think I will make a break for it when night comes, if alive. It's not night yet. The house is all fired. Goodbye, boys, if I never see you again.

NATHAN D. CHAMPION

He then dashed out of the back door of the cabin, which was already on fire. His pistol was in his belt and his Winchester in his hand, and he was bareheaded and in his stockinged feet. He loosed off one shot before a bullet struck his right arm and he died with twenty-seven more in him, several of them piercing his brave heart.

His killers read his diary, erased a mention of Canton, then pinned a card on to his blood-drenched vest. It warned: 'Cattle thieves, beware!'

Nate never had the joy of knowing that news had reached the outside, though early in the fight he had spotted two men ride by. Some of the invaders pursued them but they escaped. Unbeknown to Nate or his enemies, the two rode to Buffalo and alerted the town, which was soon humming in anger. Sheriff Angus, getting no help either from the nearby Fort McKinney, or from the National Guard, and finding the wires cut when he tried to alert the governor, promptly organised a posse, which was soon galloping out of town.

Wolcott and his men were now heading for Buffalo, having sent two of the three men Nate Champion had wounded back to Casper, and having eaten a hot meal. Morale was not exactly high, and it became lower when James Craig, one of the W.S.G.A., suddenly rode up to them shouting: 'Turn back! Turn back! Everybody in town is aroused. The rustlers are massing from every direction! Get to cover as soon as you can if you value your lives!'

The Texans under Canton and Smith wanted to go on anyway, having come such a long way to fight, but the gentlemen of the Cheyenne Club decided to retreat to the TA Ranch, where they had

above
The cabin in which Nate Champion fought off the Johnson County invaders until he could hold out no longer – and came out firing.

left
The barn where the Johnson County War ended in humiliation for the invaders, who had to be rescued by the U.S. Cavalry.

below
Frank Canton, a dangerous killer and one of the most sinister figures in the Johnson County War.

opposite
A remarkable group photograph of the Johnson County invaders.

halted a short time before, and dig in. Wolcott was now master enough of the situation to get his way.

They fortified the place well and the club members found themselves blistered and aching. A barricade about twelve by fourteen feet had been set up, followed by trenches and earthworks. They could be starved out perhaps, but otherwise were surely impregnable.

On 11 April, the fighting began, with the TA surrounded by angry settlers and small ranchers led by 'Red' Angus, then by bearded Arapahoe Brown when the sheriff returned to Buffalo to keep things humming there. On the 12th, the wires were mended and word got through to the governor. Soon the President heard that Johnson County was in a state of insurrection and, as only the W.S.G.A.'s version of events reached Washington, orders were given to rescue the would-be exterminators from their unfortunate predicament, made worse because the Texans and cattle barons were not getting on too well. For instance, Wolcott ordered one Texan to go and relieve an outpost with eight men, one of whom refused to budge. The major informed him that he was a white-livered son-of-a-bitch and that if he did not move smartly, he, the major, would personally kill him. The man went.

Colonel J. J. Horn commanding three troops of the Sixth Cavalry arrived on the scene to the profound relief of the cattlemen, though at least one Texan thought he was about to have to take on the army as well. The defenders had just finished what they feared might be their last breakfast when the welcome bugle was heard. Wolcott agreed to surrender to Horn, but not to 'that man', his description of sheriff Angus, who by now had returned. Angus himself delivered a withering blast of invective against the cattlemen and their hirelings – and the authorities. 'I had them in my grasp,' he said of the invaders, 'and they were taken from me.'

The forty-six mightily relieved men were taken away to Fort McKinney in what amounted to protective custody. Angus wanted them tried by a civilian court, but the governor, fearing for their safety, refused. Nate and Nick Ray were given a glorious funeral, and a coroner's court found that they had been murdered, but by January 1893 the case against the invaders had been dropped. Everything depended on the evidence of the two trappers, but, fearful of their lives, the pair accepted large bribes and fled the state.

The cattle barons, though they were to admit that the invasion had been illegal, felt complacently certain that they had been in the right. As for Frank Canton, he or his ghost writer uttered the following boast in an autobiography, *Frontier Trails*, published in 1930: 'We made it safe for an honest man to live in that county [Johnson County] and enjoy the fruits of his labour.' But he was by nature a writer of fiction. He described the Dawson City of 1898 as a wild, lawless town, the like of which would never be seen again. 'It was a picture of blood . . .', this in a year when, thanks to the North-West Mounted Police, not a single murder took place in the city, and precious little theft.

In the long run, the ordinary people of Johnson County were the winners of the war. The cattle barons never exercised the same control as before and their party, the Republicans, lost the elections of 1892. Those who had truly been rustlers either cut down their activities or gave up crime, and finally all sections of the community began to get along. And Nate Champion's fame remained undimmed. All those killed were remembered by the people as martyrs, but Nate was their greatest hero. Songs of the war were sung by cowhands for many years, and one of them was inspired by the diary which, along with his valour, has made him a supreme Frontier immortal.

Chapter 5

Showdowns and Shootists

Once upon a time – the time being 21 July 1865 – there really was a Hollywood-style shoot-out in the West, though it happened just after 6 pm, not at High Noon. Fourteen years later, the Gunfight at the OK Corral, fought at much closer range, was another rare example of the genre, but its facts are so disputed that it is not so perfect an example as the earlier occasion, when Wild Bill Hickok faced Dave Tutt on the Market Square of Springfield in Missouri.

Tutt was a Confederate veteran and, like Hickok, was a brave man and a skilled shot. They had fallen out over cards and, probably, over a woman's favours, and Tutt had taken Wild Bill's repeater watch in lieu of an alleged debt and boldly announced he would wear it on the square. Hickok was not the man to allow such an act and the confrontation followed.

In front of a fine crowd the two men started closing in on each other on the square and when they were some fifty yards apart, Tutt drew his pistol and fired – and missed. Wild Bill had drawn his own pistol – probably one of his Navy Colts – and fired at Tutt before the latter could recock his weapon.

Wild Bill Hickok, having killed Dave Tutt, rounds on his friends in case they have any ideas of instant revenge.

Both shots apparently sounded as one. Tutt fell dead with a bullet through his heart, by which time Hickok had spun round to where some of Tutt's friends stood watching. 'Aren't you satisfied, gentlemen?' he asked grimly. 'Put up your shootin'-irons, or there'll be more dead men here.'

The men obeyed and dispersed. Hickok was arrested the next day, but allowed out on bail. When he was finally tried he was acquitted on his reasonable plea of self-defence.

Forty-two years after this fight, Bat Masterson wrote a series of articles about the Old West in *Human Life* and used the word 'man-killers' about his fellow-gunfighters and, of course, himself. There was no slick talk about 'fast guns' in them, but good sense about men who took their time in a fight, placed their shots, kept calm and, of course, never lacked determination and the courage to kill or maim. Modern 'fast draw' experts who boast about their speed in drawing and firing have never had to shape up to a John Wesley Hardin. An electric timer is hardly so lethal an opponent. Of course, speed mattered but, as the old-timers said: 'Speed's fine, but accuracy's final.' The myth of speed is an ancient one, however. Henry Plummer in the 1860s could, according to Thomas Dimsdale in *The Vigilantes of Montana*, 'draw the pistol and discharge the five loads in three seconds'.

Ed McGivern in the early 1930s showed just what was possible with the old-time pistols. Using a Colt Peacemaker he drew and fired five shots into a man-sized target ten feet from him in just 1.6 seconds. He candidly admitted that he doubted if he could have been able to achieve anything like such a speed against another man. Fanning the pistol, McGivern achieved 1.2 seconds. (Fanning, so popular in films, was only used at close range or against a large number. The slapping or 'fanning' of the hammer to recock, with the index finger of the other hand holding the trigger pressed, is hardly calculated to promote accuracy.)

Bat Masterson summed up what was needed by the successful mankiller thus:

Samuel Colt's Pocket Pistol, Model of 1839, made at his factory at Paterson, New Jersey. A percussion-cap, single-action revolver, its trigger swings down as the hammer is cocked.

A Colt Dragoon or Old Army Model, ·44 calibre, a massive weapon in action from 1848 to *c.* 1860.

> Any man who does not possess courage, proficiency in the use of firearms, and deliberation had better make up his mind at the beginning to settle his differences in some other manner than by an appeal to the pistol. I have known men in the West whose courage could not be questioned and whose expertness with the pistol was simply marvellous, who fell easy victims before men who added deliberation to the other two qualities.

Guns

The story of the Western pistol is dominated by the name Colt. 'God created man, but it was Sam Colt's revolver that made him equal,' went the Frontier saying. Even a weakling could stand up to a man-mountain if the former knew how to handle his six-shooter.

Colt pistols were in use from 1836, the early weapons being five-shot. They saw service against the Seminoles in Florida and, in the hands of Texas Rangers, against the Comanches in Texas.

These early weapons were percussion: they had to be loaded with powder and ball, while their charge was set off by a copper cap containing fulminate of mercury. This was put on a nipple or small tube at the back of the chamber and was detonated when the hammer hit it.

The Colt Walker, named by Sam Colt for an ex-Ranger, was first produced in 1846 and was a six-shooter, a big .44 calibre gun which could send a ball over 600 yards with an original muzzle velocity of 1,500 feet per second. The 'Army' or 'Dragoon' was introduced in 1848, but it was the 'Colt's Navy revolver, model of 1851' that gunfighters decided upon. So did the British. Forty thousand were manufactured at Sam Colt's London factory and thousands were bought by the British Government and used in the Crimea.

Except in the hands of an expert, the Navy was essentially a close-range weapon (i.e. up to twenty-five yards). The Colt New Model Army appeared in 1860, two years before Sam Colt died, and by now there were also many pocket pistols on the market. In 1873 came the most famous pistol of all, the Colt Single Action Army revolver, model of 1873, the legendary Peacemaker. This .45 calibre masterpiece and its rivals had 'fixed' or metallic ammunition, the cap, ball and powder being contained in a brass or copper case, as it is today. And apart from a break from 1941–55, the Peacemaker has been in production ever since its introduction.

Remington and Smith and Wesson were among Colt's rivals, some gunfighters preferring the Smith and Wesson .44 'American' revolver to the Peacemaker. The most famous rifle was the Winchester, model of 1873, so popular that the Colt Company in 1878 rechambered a number of Peacemakers to hold its cartridge, marking each one 'Frontier Six-Shooter'.

Gunfighters tended to wear their guns in leather holsters slung on their hips, or, in some cases, waist high with butts pointing forward for cross draws. It became the fashion to wear pistols with their butts to the rear when cartridge pistols appeared, needing loops on the belt to hold the cartridges. Guns were not worn low on the leg, Hollywood style, but high on the hip. The custom of carrying two guns was more observed in the days before metallic cartridges than later, the second being a reserve; the old pistols inevitably took longer to load and were liable to jam. Two guns could be useful in a saloon brawl or against a mob, but few gunfighters were ambidextrous.

Only a handful of 'pistoleers' can be featured here, some men who have already appeared elsewhere.

'Jack' Slade

An early specimen was Joseph 'Jack' Slade (1824–64), who fought in the war against Mexico (1846–48), then, after a spell in Kansas, became a line superintendent of the Central Overland California and Pike's Peak Express Company. He was a likeable enough man when sober, but took to drinking in a spectacular way and could be guaranteed to fill a church on Sunday when the cry 'Slade's drunk!' was heard. Every pew was full as men hastened to find 'a hole to hide in'.

Slade believed in revenge Old Testament style. One enemy, Jules Bene, who had tried to kill him, was later tied to a fence post and plugged full of holes before Slade put him out of his misery by placing the barrel of his pistol in Bene's mouth and pulling the trigger. It is said that Slade then cut off Bene's ears, pickled them and put one to use as a watch fob.

Mark Twain came across him and wrote about him in *Roughing It*:

> Slade was a matchless marksman with a navy revolver. The legends say that one morning at Rocky Ridge, when he was feeling comfortable, he saw a man approaching who had offended him some days before – observe the fine memory he had for matters like that – and, 'Gentlemen,' said Slade, drawing, 'it is a good twenty-five yard shot – I'll clip the third button on his coat!' Which he did. The bystanders all admired it. And they all attended the funeral too.

below, far left
The classic Winchester ·44–40 calibre rifle, Model of 1873, the so-called 'gun that won the West', a perhaps pardonable exaggeration.

below, left
A Sharps Buffalo rifle with its heavy octagonal barrel. Made in ·50–·45 and some smaller calibres, it was first introduced in 1874.

below, right
An extra-fine quality Model 1876 Winchester, an example of the famous 'One of a Thousand', said to be perfect in every respect.

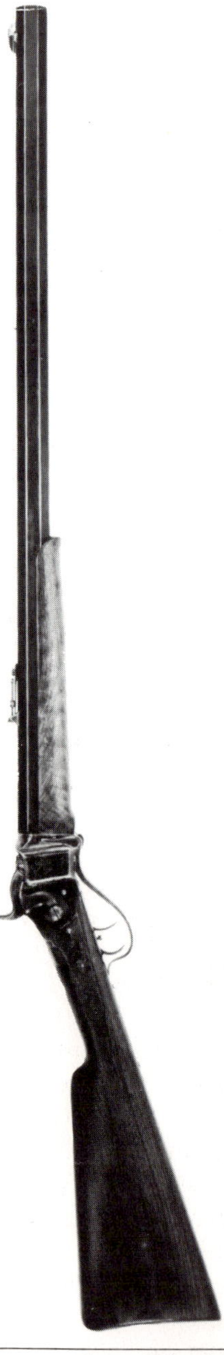

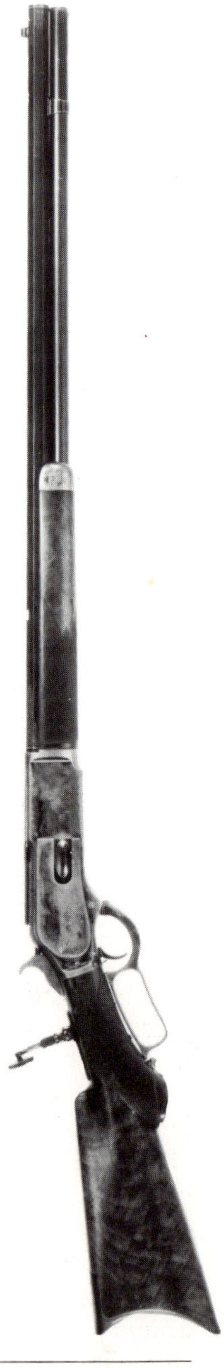

Slade's career went downhill and in Montana, after trying his hand at ranching, drink got the better of him and he was finally hanged by vigilantes. They had been quite tolerant with him for his habit of shooting up the town, Virginia City, when in liquor, but after a final admonition of 'Get your horse and go home' had no effect – he headed straight for the bar again – they strung him up from a crossbeam of a corral gate. He had charm when sober . . .

William P. Longley

William P. Longley (1851–78) had less charm. He came of age in the grim period of Texas' history after the Civil War and soon fell out with the hated state police, who, as we have seen, were mostly ex-slaves. That can hardly excuse his exploits: when he was on trial for his life in 1877, the press claimed he had killed thirty-two men, mostly blacks. So did he. He was finally tried for murder in Texas, his victim being a man who had shot one of his cousins. When he was waiting to die on the gallows in front of 4,000 interested spectators he looked around and – accurately, for he was a loner – said: 'I see a good many enemies around and mighty few friends.'

He had a cruel death, for he was given a long drop – twelve feet – and when the rope slipped his feet were on the ground. He was hauled up and dropped again and, eleven minutes later, was pronounced dead.

John Wesley Hardin

John Wesley Hardin (1853–1895) had much the same background as Longley, who disliked the younger Hardin, his rival in ill-fame. By 1878, when he was imprisoned, he claimed to have dispatched forty-four men, and there is no reason to suppose he was indulging in Frontier boasting, for Hardin was a killer. Again, the poisonous atmosphere in Reconstruction Texas does not excuse him. By 1871, when he was in Abilene, having come up the trail with a herd owned by one Columbus Carol, he had killed twelve men, and he was to kill eight more in Kansas. His most notorious exploit was the shooting of a man

The Remington 'Elliot' Deringer, firing a ·41 calibre rimfire cartridge. It was made from 1867 to 1888.

All the guns on this and the previous spread, excepting the Deringer, are on display at the Winchester Gun Museum, New Haven, Connecticut.

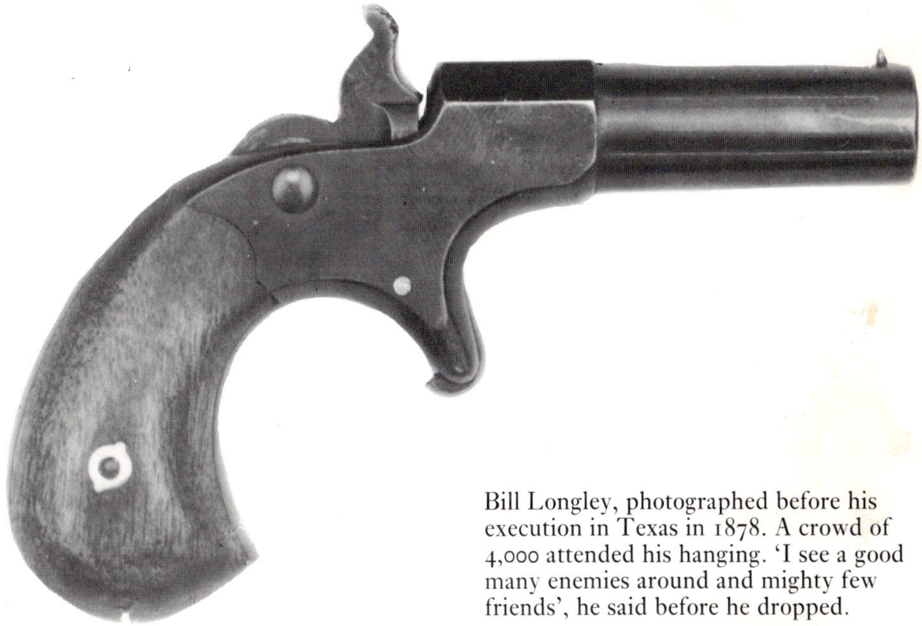

Bill Longley, photographed before his execution in Texas in 1878. A crowd of 4,000 attended his hanging. 'I see a good many enemies around and mighty few friends', he said before he dropped.

left
John Wesley Hardin, a ruthless and notorious killer who served a long term in jail and was later murdered in El Paso.

below
Wes Hardin leaving Abilene in a hurry.

opposite
Lawman Jeff Milton called Wes Hardin a liar to his face and lived to get an apology. Milton was the finest type of lawman: there were not many of them.

Wes Hardin's single-action Army ·45 revolver.

in the next room in his hotel. Hardin was reading a paper, sitting on his bed, when his neighbour's snoring upset him. Marshal Hickok, who had been on friendly terms with the young man until that moment, was not amused and headed for the hotel, but Hardin was too quick for him and escaped in his undershirt, Texas bound.

Finally, the Rangers cornered him in a train at Pensacola Junction, Florida. Hardin was not on form that day, for his pistol got jammed in his braces and he was arrested without getting off a shot.

He was jailed and at last released in 1894, his adored wife having died in the meantime. He had studied law in prison and opened a law office in El Paso, Texas, but the heart had gone out of him and he spent more time in saloons than in his office. Finally, a local lawman, John Selman, shot him in the back of the head in the Acme Saloon. Selman had made an evil name for himself in the aftermath of the Lincoln County War on the wrong side of the law – what law there was – and now he was to say that Hardin had a chance to see him in a mirror over the bar. He was acquitted for his cold-blooded murder, presumably because he had shot a man who had once been a notorious killer. Fortunately, the dead man had written a fascinating autobiography, which, for all its inaccuracies and special pleading, is a fine document. (Some allege he did not write it.)

Clay Allison

Yet another Texan 'bad man to fool with' was the notorious Clay Allison (1840–87), though he had some excuse. He was discharged from the Tennessee Light Infantry, having sustained a blow on his skull which is said to have made him partially epileptic and partially maniacal. He became a cowboy and rancher and acquired a dangerous reputation, especially in drink. Legends abound about him, including the story that he once rode down the streets of a cowtown wearing only a pair of six-guns. He once led a lynching party against a mass murderer whose crimes apparently included infanticide – the man's own daughter – and when the man, named Kennedy, had died, he cut off his head and rode to his favourite saloon with it. He once indulged in a fast draw contest with a gunman named Mace Bowman, who got the better of him, so Allison suggested stripping down to their underwear and shooting at each other's feet to see who danced best under fire. Incredibly, neither was hurt.

Allison arranged to fight a naked duel in a grave, with both men using Bowie knives, as a way of settling a dispute. Whoever staggered out at the end of the duel could engrave the tombstone in no doubt exquisite taste. Alas, for posterity, Clay met a wretched fate before this epic contest could be fought. He was on his way home from Pecos, Texas, with a wagonload of supplies for his ranch, where he lived with his wife, whom he had married in 1878, and his two daughters. A sack of grain fell off and he seems to have toppled from the wagon trying to retrieve it as it fell. A wagon wheel went over his neck and he died soon after in agony, a bizarre fate for a gunfighter whose career was often bizarre.

Sam Bass

A less remarkable but more famous badman was Sam Bass (1851–78), who had the good fortune to have an excellent song written around his not very successful efforts as an outlaw, 'Sam Bass was born in Indiana'. Like others, he found life dull and opted for crime, though horse-racing was his major passion. He, a stronger character called Joel Collins, and some confederates pulled off one successful train robbery of a Union Pacific train in Nebraska before Bass formed his own gang and carried out some hold-ups in Texas. He was freer with his (or, rather, other people's) money than some outlaws, but the result was the same as it was with most others. In his case, the Texas Rangers ran him to ground at Round Rock in 1878 after one of his gang had betrayed him. After being wounded by a Ranger's bullet and captured the next day in the brush, he died on his twenty-seventh birthday.

Tom Horn

Bass's story is a straightforward case of a youngster going to the bad, but Tom Horn's remains controversial to this day. His early life before he became a hired gun was an action-packed one, for he served as a scout in the Apache Wars under the great Chief of Scouts Al Sieber, who composed a glowing testimonial about him when he later fell into deep trouble. Wrote the once legendary and now too little-known Sieber: 'A more faithful or better worker or a more honorable man I never met in my life . . . I can never believe that the jolly, jovial, honorable and whole-souled Tom Horn I knew was a low-down miserable murderer.'

So what happened to turn a youthful hero who could speak Apache and was a notable leader of Apache scouts into – so his enemies said – a despicable killer?

Perhaps after the excitement of the Apache wars it was hard to settle down to mining, his first occupation after they ended. He became a Pinkerton detective, then, probably, a range detective, which must have been easy work for one used to tracking Apaches in the desert. He was in the Spanish-American War, but invalided out with fever, then he returned to Wyoming, where he had first worked in 1894. He became a 'stock detective', which might be interpreted by neutrals as a hired gun and by enemies as a thief killer. He was approved of by the cattle barons, for whom he represented a one-man invasion, a small-scale version of their botched efforts in the Johnson County War, and he was clearly well paid for his services, but whereas in the 'war' it is easy to take sides and support the little men of Johnson County, what happened later is harder to determine.

above
John Selman, killer of Wes Hardin, shot his man from behind. The jury acquitted him of the murder that it was.

right
Clay Allison was violent enough to terrify most men on the Frontier.

above, left
Sam Bass was born in Indiana, as the song about him begins. Here he is aged sixteen.

above
Getting the drop, as pictured by Frederic Remington.

It is harder still because Horn had the Frontier habit of exaggeration and he may have inspired much of his awesome reputation by his own boasting.

His downfall, which divides opinion to this day in and out of Wyoming, began early in 1901. Two families of homesteaders, the Millers and the Nickells, had ceased to be friendly, and when Jim Miller stabbed Kels Nickell dislike turned to hatred. Nickell, however, survived. His fourteen-year-old son Willie was less lucky, for he was ambushed and shot not far from home.

There had been local hostility to Kels Nickell, for he had introduced sheep to a cattle range and Wyoming's feelings about sheepmen lasted longer than those in other states: the last major clash occurred as late as 1909. However, at the inquest, there was no evidence against the most likely suspects, the Millers, who seemed anxious to place the blame on Tom Horn. In his job he was everybody's prime suspect. The boy had been big for his age, the light was dim at dawn. Perhaps Horn, acting for the cattle bosses, had shot the boy mistaking him for his father.

The evidence was nil and the case against Horn was too feeble to be brought to court; moreover, a lady friend of his, Glendolene Kimmell, who had been 'born and reared midst the comforts and refinements of civilization', as she wrote in her excellent statement on his behalf after his death, was quite prepared to state that the Millers wanted suspicion thrown onto Tom: they told her so.

It seemed, however, as if the case would be closed from lack of hard facts when on to the scene came the sinister Joe Lafors, currently a deputy US marshal but famous as a stock detective. He began trying to crack the case.

opposite
Tom Horn, executed in Wyoming for the murder of a youth, was probably framed. He is holding the rope which is said to have hanged him.

below
Jefferson Randolph 'Soapy' Smith was a master con-man in Colorado and at Skagway in Alaska. His nickname came from his trick of selling shaving-soap sticks apparently laden with paper money.

To gain his confidence, Lafors told Horn about an opening in Montana as a stock detective. Tom got as far as Omaha, Nebraska, where, breaking his journey, he got drunk and, as always, changed from a quiet citizen to a braggart. He lost his belongings and had to return. While collecting things together at his friend John Coble's ranch, he had a note from Lafors asking if he would meet him in Cheyenne.

Horn broke his journey back at Laramie and once again got drunk, so that when he met Lafors in Cheyenne he was drunker than ever. By the time Lafors had managed to get him to the marshal's office, he was scarcely able to move and not much better at talking. But talk he did to deadly effect, for he described in considerable and boastful detail how he had killed young Willie, while a hidden stenographer took it all down. For this 'confession' he was arrested, tried and convicted, plead as he might that he had merely been bragging and that the stenographer had rigged the evidence.

His friends vainly tried to save him, but his own words hanged him on 20 November 1902, aged forty-three. It was reported that he died without squealing, to the relief of many respectable citizens, but the chances are he had nothing to squeal about and that he was 'railroaded' to the gallows. He was too experienced a bounty hunter to make such a mistake, besides it is hard not to believe Glendolene Kimmell's long account. No doubt as a hired gun there were plenty of questionable events in his life, but not the one that ended it. Unless new evidence comes to light, however, the case stays open, still hotly debated in Wyoming.

Billy the Kid

Arguments still rage over Billy the Kid, too. He has already been featured for his part in the Lincoln County War, but the most dramatic moments for him were yet to come. Fortunately, the real Billy is beginning to emerge strongly, even his boyhood, thanks to specialists like Robert Mullin and Waldo Koop, following in the footsteps of the great historian of the Lincoln County War, namely Colonel Maurice Fulton.

Mullin has conclusively proved in his monograph, *The Boyhood of Billy the Kid*, that the notorious outlaw's early years were singularly quiet. It needed circumstances to cause any lethal qualities to erupt. Popular novels, rushed into print as soon as he died, followed newspaper articles of his own day in 'improving' Billy's life, and Pat Garrett's *The Authentic Life of Billy the Kid* (1882), ghosted by one Ashman Upson, was little better. So thousands believed that twelve-year-old

Billy murdered a 'filthy loafer' who had insulted his mother, using a pocket knife whose blade dripped 'with gore' after the deed. And a story of how Billy had routed an Indian band with his pistol emitting 'a stream of death-laden fire' was assumed to be fact, not the fiction it was.

There are mysteries still. Billy was either born in Indiana or New York in 1859 and his surname was McCarty or Bonney. His first name was Henry. He, his brother Joe and his mother settled later in Kansas at Wichita, then went to Silver City, New Mexico, where his mother remarried a miner named Antrim. Henry was no trouble to his teachers and apparently performed in amateur theatricals!

His first brush with the law was not a \$70 robbery, as his legend has it. In fact, Henry McCarty and another boy agreed to hide some clothes that a character called 'Sombrero Jack' had stolen from two Chinese. The local sheriff, no doubt as a lesson, put Henry in jail, the young 'criminal' refusing to name his helper. His nerves got the better of him and he escaped to Arizona where he worked as a ranch hand. Again contrary to legend, his life was uneventful. He was now 'Kid' or Kid Antrim.

On 17 August 1877 he killed his first man, burly Frank 'Windy' Cahill who delighted in bullying the slight Kid. One day he taunted him, calling him a pimp and a son-of-a-bitch and the two began wrestling. The Kid was thrown, drew a gun on his tormentor, and killed him, one watcher later saying that the boy had no choice. He was arrested all the same, but managed to escape by unknown means.

What happened next when, as William Bonney, he signed on with the ambitious, good-natured Englishman, John Tunstall, has been fully described in the previous chapter, Billy's part in the Lincoln County War being left at the end of the five-day battle in Lincoln.

With the war virtually over, the more vicious of Dolan's supporters went on the rampage in the county, looting, killing, robbing and raping. Billy and some of his friends formed a gang of their own, rustling but not raping.

above
A picture of Billy the Kid which is now thought to be authentic.

right
Wildly inaccurate dime novels appeared regularly about most of the leading Wild Western characters, either during their lives or after their deaths.

opposite
Billy the Kid, complete with two right hands, perpetrates a mythical killing.

RYE

Such was the anarchy that the President sent General Lew Wallace to New Mexico, just when his book, *Ben Hur*, was almost finished. The unfortunate Civil War veteran was meant to restore order.

Billy decided that he would give himself up and testify against other combatants in the war: it might help balance the string of murder warrants outstanding against him. The startled Wallace had a letter from the Kid asking for an interview. At a secret meeting Billy got his pardon promised him and went into technical custody. His testimony helped have the arch villain Dolan indicted, but the latter had too many influential friends to be touched, and when a lawyer questioned Billy's pardon, he decided to slip away and return to crime. He and his gang lifted many cattle from John Chisum, Billy always feeling that the cattle king owed him money for his part in the Lincoln County War. He once threatened the unarmed Chisum with a gun, but presumably remembered just in time that killing a cattle baron was suicidal, as his boys had a way of extracting rapid revenge.

Now it was 1880 and Billy's gang was too successful for the authorities. An erstwhile friend of his, Pat Garrett, now sheriff of Lincoln County, and an impressive-looking man of six feet four inches, went after the gang. On 19 December, when they were riding to Fort Sumner, Tom O'Folliard at their head was killed, and four days later, Garrett and his men cornered Billy and his remaining four comrades at Stinking Springs. Charles Bowdre was killed, and then the other four surrendered.

Billy was tried in April 1881 for sheriff Brady's murder. He was the only one of the participants in the Lincoln County War to be tried and convicted of a killing. He had, of course, been one of the killers, and was sentenced to death, the date of execution being set as 13 May. He was confined in the county jail, once the Dolan and Murphy store of ill repute.

On 28 April, Pat Garrett was either collecting taxes or – a nicer story – arranging for carpenters to build Billy's scaffold, when the Kid achieved a masterpiece. While Robert Olinger, one of his two guards, was supervising prisoners as they ate in a restaurant over the road from the jail, Billy asked the other guard, J. W. Bell, to take him to the privy. Returning, Billy swiftly slipped the handcuffs off his small hands – he had used the trick before – and knocked Bell down using his shackles as a weapon. Then he shot him. The most plausible explanation of how he got a gun is that one had been hidden in the privy by his friend Sam Corbet, who had been allowed to visit Billy daily. Sam could have slipped him a note with the single word 'privy' on it.

below
Pat Garrett, who killed Billy the Kid and later co-operated in a biography of him.

opposite
General Lew Wallace, author of *Ben Hur*, who was sent by the President to try to restore order in Lincoln County.

Now Billy seized a shotgun in Garrett's office and waited by a window for Olinger to come running after hearing the shot. 'Hullo, Bob!' shouted Billy and fired as his captor looked up. Then he smashed the gun and threw it down beside the dead deputy. Later, Billy the Kid, still shackled on one leg, rode away laughing, having shaken hands all round. It was reported that he apologised to the dead Bell, but not to Olinger, whom he disliked. 'You are not going to round me up again,' he said, touching the body with his boot.

Even the *New Mexican*, the organ of the anti-Tunstall-McSween forces, could not begrudge admiration for Billy's supreme coup, while his many American and Mexican admirers rejoiced at his escape. But he could not evade Pat Garrett for long. On 14 July 1881, the tall lawman rode to Fort Sumner, having heard a report that Billy was there, and with Garrett rode two deputies.

At the fort, Garrett called at the cabin of a rancher named Pete Maxwell, who he knew would probably know where Billy was. He left his deputies outside and entered Maxwell's bedroom.

Billy had been dancing and was now feeling hungry. He had been told there was a quarter of butchered steer on Maxwell's porch and walked there, hatless and shoeless. He saw the deputies, drew his gun – those who later alleged he was unarmed insult the memory of a highly professional outlaw – and quietly entered Maxwell's room to find out who the men were. He failed to see the man sitting on the edge of Maxwell's bed.

'Who are they, Pete?' Billy asked and Maxwell whispered: 'That's him!' Billy started for the door calling: 'Quien es? Quien es?' ('Who's that?'), then Garrett drew his pistol and killed him.

Following an old Spanish custom, the local people took it in turns to stay with Billy's body and pray for

opposite, above
Billy's killing of Robert Olinger, as pictured in Pat Garrett's biography of The Kid, a ghosted book more accurate pictorially than in its text.

opposite, below
The Lincoln County Courthouse after restoration in the 1930s.

above
The death of Billy the Kid, another illustration from Garrett's biography.

him before the funeral. And after it, he was buried in the government cemetery inside the fort. As for Pat Garrett, though his exploit made his name, it did not make him over-popular. However, he held good jobs at first until a ranch he had acquired in New Mexico failed and he began to drink too much. Finally, he feuded with a neighbour who killed him in 1908.

As for Billy, he was an even greater legend in death than he had been the last months of his life. The myth that he had killed twenty-one men for every one of his years stuck, yet the facts were otherwise. Acting on his own he is known to have killed only one man, the bully Cahill, though he helped bury at least five others in the 'war'. Perhaps in all he killed less than ten.

There was nothing maniacal about him: he is not to be compared to Hardin, for instance, as a killer, and if he was no Robin Hood, there were many who genuinely liked and loved him. Circumstances hardened him and it would be foolish to pretend that there was not already a streak of ruthlessness in him, waiting to be tapped. But the reader who has followed the account of the atmosphere in Lincoln County, the war that followed the killing of Tunstall, and the desperate times immediately after it, will surely judge Billy the Kid far less harshly than many of the characters in this book.

Shoot-outs

To end this chapter, there are accounts of five gunfights to add to those already related, to show more examples of what the shoot-outs of the Old West were really like.

Luke Short was a well-dressed saloon owner, gambler and gunfighter who had useful friends on the Dodge City Police force. However, his best-known shoot-out occurred in Fort Worth, Texas, in 1887, where he had moved from Dodge City after some trouble with the city's administration. In Fort Worth he found himself up against a protection racket – and long-haired marshal Jim Courtright. Matters came to a climax on 8 February 1887, when Short was told that the marshal wanted him on the street. He left his White Elephant Saloon casually and stood before Courtright with his thumbs tucked into the armholes of his waistcoat, then he lowered his hands, apparently smoothing out the waistcoat.

Courtright warned him not to draw a gun and, as if hurt by the suggestion, Short replied: 'I'm not trying to pull a gun. I haven't got a gun there, see!'

Though he pulled at his coat, Courtright correctly took no chances and went for his pistol, while Short also drew and loosed off a wild shot. Texas legend has it that his bullet hit Courtright's thumb as he was drawing and cocking his weapon. Frantically, the marshal tried to shift the pistol to his left hand, but Luke Short was easily able to plug him with three bullets. But an examination of Courtright's pistol showed the cylinder was jammed and would not have turned. The shift may be myth! And Luke? He died of dropsy in Fort Worth in 1893.

A gunfight where the loser, a crack shot, failed to take his time and calmly place his shots happened in Dodge City in the Long Branch Saloon on 5 April 1879. The crack shot, buffalo hunter Levi Richardson, fell out with gambler Frank 'Cock-Eyed' Loving. The pair started shooting at close range after exchanging insults, Richardson firing first and missing. Frank's first shot went wide, too, and he retreated behind the pot-bellied stove in the middle of the room. Richardson fired three more shots which all missed, then 'Cock-Eyed' Frank stopped and stood his ground and shot Richardson in the left breast. As the wounded man tottered backwards, he was hit once more in the chest, but Richardson got off one more shot before he fell to the floor. By now marshal Charlie Bassett and a deputy had arrived to disarm Loving, and they stopped Richardson firing a last shot from the floor before he died.

Incredibly, none of the onlookers had been hit. Loving was found to have been acting in self-defence by the jury. His .44 Remington proved to be empty after the fight and in Richardson's six-shooter there were five empty cartridges and one live round. In other words, eleven shots had been exchanged and only two hits had been registered in a short-range fight. It was not the sort of fight which would have been admired by Bat Masterson and other noted 'man-killers'.

It is worth noting that many gunfighters only loaded five bullets into their pistols, letting the hammer rest in the empty chamber. Wyatt Earp was a five bullet man, but forgot to obey his own rule once at Wichita in the Custom House Saloon:

Luke Short, dapper and dangerous. Like many other Westerners, he enjoyed dressing in the height of fashion though few looked as elegant as he did.

. . . his revolver slipped from its holster and in falling to the floor the hammer, which was resting on the cap, is supposed to have struck the chair causing a discharge of one of the barrels [chambers]. The ball passed through his coat, struck the north wall then glanced off and passed out through the ceiling. It was a narrow escape and the occurrence got up a lively stampede from the room. One of the demoralised was under the impression that some one had fired through the window from the outside.

One of the finest-looking Western lawmen was Dallas Stoudenmire, the tall, strong-jawed marshal of El Paso, Texas, the town he tamed. He had a long-standing feud with the Manning brothers, the town's chief racketeers, but went on the bottle when certain citizens made both sides sign a peace pledge to avoid bloodshed. His drinking lost him his job, then, on 18 September 1882, he decided to confront the Mannings. With ex-policeman and friend Walt Jones, he went to the Coliseum Saloon where two of the brothers were, Jim by the bar and 'Doc' playing billiards. Jim left to fetch the third brother, Frank, while 'Doc' put down his cue and began arguing with Stoudenmire.

The argument culminated in both men going for their pistols. Walt Jones attempted to calm things down but was pushed aside by his friend. This waste of valuable seconds gave 'Doc' Manning time to shoot the ex-marshal with his double-action .44, though, luckily, the ball struck his right breast pocket, where it lodged in his pocket book and a bunch of letters. But Manning fired another shot and hit Dallas in the left breast.

He staggered back, but his gun was out and he shot 'Doc' in his right arm above the elbow. At once, Manning dropped his pistol and flung himself on Dallas, wrapping his arms round him, despite his painful wound, in a great bear-hug to stop him from shooting again. There followed a veritable *dance macabre* between the big ex-marshal and the short racketeer, a dance that finally led the pair out into the street, where Jim Manning suddenly returned with a .45. He fired – and smashed a barber's pole, then more calmly aimed and hit Dallas in the head. That was the end of him. 'Doc' pulled himself free, then seized one of the dead man's guns and started battering the corpse's head until he was dragged away by onlookers. The brothers were tried and cleared, while those who recalled Dallas Stoudenmire in his prime reckoned that drink was his worst enemy. The 'man-killer' needed all his faculties intact.

Two gunfights set in Arizona end this chapter. The first is the most famous of them all, the Gunfight at the OK Corral, which remains highly controversial because of widely differing interpretations, not only of what happened that day in Tombstone, but also of the characters of the Earps, especially of Wyatt Earp. His importance in the story of the Wild West was greatly distorted and exaggerated by his previously mentioned biographer, Stuart Lake, so it should be noted that in his own day his fame rested mainly on the Tombstone episode. His record in Kansas was by no means an indifferent one, but he never held a senior post there, whereas Lake has him a town-tamer more potent than Tom Smith and Wild Bill Hickok combined – and a Sir Galahad of the West into the bargain.

Tombstone had become a town by 1879, two years after a prospector named Ed Schieffelin found a vast silver lode at the spot. It got its name because Ed had been prospecting for stones (quartz) in wild Apache country and a friend told him: 'Reckon the only stone you're gonna find'll be your tombstone.' Which gave him an idea for a name . . .

left
Wyatt Earp, head of a controversial band of brothers.

below, left
Morgan Earp, who died playing pool in a saloon, killed in the aftermath of the fight at the OK Corral.

below
Virgil Earp was hit in the calf at the OK Corral by a bullet from Billy Clanton.

By 1880, Wyatt, Virgil, James and Morgan Earp, along with various wives and mistresses, were in the booming town, though James, nursing a Civil War wound, was to take no part in the coming action. Wyatt's gun-toting dentist friend arrived, the notorious 'Doc' Holliday, who was tubercular and deservedly unpopular. He is said to have saved Wyatt Earp's life from a mob of drunken cowboys on one occasion.

In October 1880, Virgil, by then a deputy city marshal, took over the top job when his boss, Fred White, was killed. Wyatt was busy in the saloon and gambling trades, managing to fit in some work for Wells Fargo and, later, as deputy sheriff of Pima County. Their chief rivals in the locality were soon to be the ranching and cowboy element, who resented the mining community, who in turn regarded cowboys as synonymous with rustlers. The Earp clan was officially in the middle, but a series of events turned them against the longer-established cattlemen, in particular the outfits of two families, the Clantons and the McLaurys, whose enemies claimed they were rustlers. It seems

below
There was no love lost between John Behan, sheriff of Cochise County, and the Earps.

opposite
A rooster fight in Tombstone in the 1880s.

clear that they were ranchers *and* rustlers.

As this is the story of the fight and the immediate events before it, the long countdown to it must be omitted. But the fact that the cowboy-rustler element had a friend in John Behan, sheriff of the newly formed Cochise County, must be noted, for he needed cowboy votes. He and the Earps were at loggerheads. Behan was to arrest Holliday on reasonable suspicion of killing a stage driver and the Earps were to be accused – by report – of masterminding the robbery using inside knowledge. Tension mounted until the Clanton and McLaury outfits wanted the Earps out of the way, and vice versa. Then Virgil arrested two of Behan's deputies for robbing a stage in September 1881, while Frank McLaury openly challenged Morgan to a shoot-out which he refused.

On 25 October, 'Doc' Holliday insulted Ike Clanton at a lunch counter. Ike was soon retreating,

right
Billy Breakenridge, John Behan's deputy, and a resolute critic of Wyatt Earp for many years after the gunfight at the OK Corral.

with Wyatt, Morgan and Virgil watching him in less than friendly fashion as he fled, begging Morgan not to shoot him in the back.

After a night of booze and cards, Ike, his courage restored, was loudly uttering threats on the street, later carrying a rifle and six-shooter to back them up. He was hit over the head with the barrel of Virgil's pistol and fell on his knees, stunned. After an exchange of insults Virgil arrested him for carrying firearms in the city limits. Morgan and Wyatt were soon on the spot and, later, Ike having been fined, Tom McLaury received the barrel of Wyatt Earp's pistol on his head and was left moaning in the street. The hatred between the two factions was now volcanic. As for 'Doc' Holliday, he spent the night before the gunfight playing poker.

Now it was 26 October. News was brought to the Earps that their enemies, Ike and Billy Clanton, Frank and Tom McLaury, and Billy Claiborne, were at the OK Corral.

Wyatt and Morgan started out to be joined by 'Doc', carrying a shotgun. Behan, in a barber shop, saw a crowd gathering and sought out Virgil. He asked him to disarm their enemies rather than fight them, but Virgil took no notice. Behan then said he would disarm 'the boys'.

He met Morgan and 'Doc', then Virgil came up, carrying a shotgun, as Behan noted. He then found Frank McLaury, holding a horse. He would not give up his guns and the pair walked to Fly's Photographic Gallery, outside which were the Clantons, Tom McLaury and Claiborne. Ike and Tom showed him they carried no guns; the rest refused to give up theirs unless the Earps were disarmed.

With the five in seemingly unwarlike mood, Behan asked them to come to his office, then the Earps came into view in line abreast and fully armed. Behan ran to halt them but was brushed aside by Virgil, who had deputised his brothers and Holliday as assistant marshals. They were in frock coats; Wyatt drew his pistol from under his and slid it into a pocket specially lined with wax-rubbed canvas for a quick draw.

The fight took place outside the corral on Fremont Street in front of Fly's gallery, with the Clantons lined up against a house and the Earps about six to eight feet away from them. Behan disappeared behind Fly's house to be joined by Billy Claiborne, and later claimed the fight started by Wyatt saying: 'You sons of bitches, you have been looking for a fight, and now you can have one.' Wyatt's version had Virgil ordering the men to give up their arms and Billy Clanton and Frank McLaury dropping their hands to their guns. So Virgil shouted: 'Hold, I don't mean that; I have come to disarm you.'

Billy Clanton called: 'Don't shoot men, I don't want to fight,' while Tom McLaury opened his coat, indicating he was unarmed.

The fight began, probably with Wyatt and Billy Clanton shooting first. Wyatt shot Frank McLaury as the most dangerous man present in his opinion and hit him in the stomach – he got off one shot before he staggered away. Billy Clanton shot at Wyatt, then the battle became general.

Ike rushed up to Wyatt and grabbed his left arm. Wyatt told him: 'The fight has now commenced; go to fighting, or get away.' Ike ran, narrowly avoiding a blast from 'Doc' Holliday's shotgun.

Meanwhile, Tom McLaury had attempted to grab Frank's Winchester from its saddle scabbard and used the horse as cover. Morgan shot Billy Clanton in the right arm, then the chest, and he fell back against Fly's place trying to get his pistol into action. Now Frank's horse reared and exposed brother Tom, who received a blast from Holliday's shotgun that killed him. The badly wounded Billy managed to put a bullet in Virgil's calf, while the dying Frank fired at 'Doc', who also fired at him. But it was Morgan who killed Frank McLaury, whose dying shot had skinned Holliday's hip and sent his holster flying.

Billy fired his last shot and hit Morgan's shoulder: as he fell, he shot Billy. So did Wyatt, and the game Billy Clanton lay on the ground, mortally wounded.

Suddenly there was silence, broken by Fly rushing out with his rifle and disarming Billy Clanton, whose last brave words were: 'Give me some more cartridges.'

It had taken less than a minute. Three men were dead, three more were seriously wounded, and two men had not been hit, Ike Clanton, who had run away, and Wyatt Earp.

With tension at boiling point in Tombstone, the Earps were exonerated in a thirty-day court hearing, though the judge did not like the enlistment of Virgil's brothers and 'Doc' as deputies. Many disliked

above
John H. 'Doc' Holliday, the notorious gunfighting dentist and friend of Wyatt Earp.

opposite, above
Newman H. Clanton, leader of the cowboy faction in Tombstone.

opposite, below
A modern stone on the grave of Doc Holliday at Glenwood Springs, Colorado.

the whole brood. Virgil Earp was later crippled for life with buckshot in his side by an unknown avenger, while Morgan was killed playing pool in March 1882, again by an unknown hand. Wyatt suspected Pete Spence and Frank Stilwell, and later killed Stilwell when he met him beside the train bearing Morgan's body back to their parents' home in California. Stilwell allegedly tried to kill Wyatt, but was soon dead beside the tracks with six bullets in him. As for Wyatt Earp, he died in bed, aged eighty. Somewhere between the St. George of his 'biographer' Lake and the monster portrayed by some modern revisionist historians is a very flawed, but interesting, human being waiting to be revealed nearly a century after his most notorious feat.

In striking contrast to the famous gunfight between two bands of gunfighters, whose motives were both suspect to say the least, is a lesser known but greater feat; indeed, there is hardly anything in the entire history of the West to touch it for sheer, swift drama.

It happened at Holbrook, Arizona, in 1887, the combatants being Commodore Perry Owens and the Blevins gang. Though the gunfight took place during the Pleasant Valley War, that murderous feud mentioned briefly in the last chapter, it was only incidentally part of it.

Holbrook was a notorious spot in the late 1880s, but on the afternoon of 4 September 1887 it was peaceful enough. The only significant thing to have happened was the arrival of a cattle thief in town, one Andy Blevins, known in Arizona as Andy Cooper. In a saloon he was busy boasting how he had killed one of the Tewksbury supporters and another man only two days earlier, Andy being a Graham adherent in the deadly feud that was raging. After his boasting he went home to mother.

That afternoon, the new sheriff of Apache County rode into Holbrook on official business. His name was Commodore Perry Owens because his father, a romantically minded admirer of the old naval hero, Commodore Perry, had thought of this way of perpetuating the name. Not that the people of Holbrook were concerned with that, for they were busy gazing at – and being startled by – their new sheriff, especially those who were looking forward to some law and order in the area.

Owens left his horse at Brown and Kinder's Livery Stable, then began to look Holbrook over. Few of those who gazed at him could know that he was a rugged product of cattle drives out of Texas, and their first glimpse of him was scarcely encouraging. He simply didn't look right. His hair trailed down below his shoulders, which was all right a decade earlier in the days of Wild Bill Hickok, but looked wrong in 1887. And his face was

decidedly pleasant and scarcely lined. He wore chaps which were ostentatiously decorated with far too many ornaments, some felt, while his Colt was worn on his left hip with its butt forward, again an out-of-date style. His Winchester inspired confidence, though, and so did his bearing and the look on his face. But the watchers could not have any idea just how good a shot and how courageous this dude-like apparition was.

His arrival in town was deliberate, not accidental. He knew that Andy Cooper was in the vicinity of Holbrook and had decided to come into town and try and make an arrest, not for taking part in the feud that was raging, but for stealing Navaho horses from the reservation.

Andy used an alias because of a murder in Texas. He got a fine welcome home from his mother, also the other Blevinses, his brother Johnny and kid brother Houston, who was sixteen. Mose Roberts, his brother-in-law, was also at home, along with Johnny's wife, as well as a Mrs Gladden and her nine-year-old daughter.

Johnny Blevins had noted Owens arriving at the livery stable and had promptly warned Andy, who had also seen the long haired lawman ride into town. The two men hastened home.

Owens carefully cleaned his six-shooter until a local politician and sheepman alerted him that Andy Blevins was about to leave town. Owens quickly reassembled his gun, seized his Winchester and, after leaving instructions that his horse should be ready for him, walked away from the stable.

He approached the Blevins' house, which stood fifteen feet back from the street, and saw Andy Blevins, or Cooper as he styled

himself, speedily saddling a horse. When he spotted the sheriff he bolted indoors.

Owens walked steadily up onto the porch and saw four men including Cooper through a window. He ordered Cooper to come out and the rustler slowly pushed the door open with his left hand. In his right was a pistol.

As if that was not enough, Johnny Blevins opened the side door off the porch. This placed the sheriff between the two brothers. With death inevitable if he made the slightest misjudgement, Owens stared at Andy Cooper, only too well aware that if he took his eyes off the rustler for a split second, he would be killed. That Andy failed to act remains a mystery. Presumably, his nerves were less steady than the piercing-eyed sheriff's.

'Cooper, I want you,' said Owens.

'What do you want with me?' asked Andy.

'I have a warrant for you,' Owens replied evenly.

Andy played for time and asked: 'What warrant?'

'The same warrant for horse-stealing I told you about some time ago,' Owens reminded him.

Cooper optimistically asked Owens to wait while he saw about the matter, but the sheriff cut in swiftly with, 'You must come at once.'

What happened next was reported in the St. Johns *Herald* on 8 September 1887, also at the inquest, where Mrs Blevins and her daughter-in-law were fatuously to claim that Andy Cooper was unarmed.

'I won't go,' Andy told Owens and both men fired, Owens being unharmed and Cooper falling backwards, with a mortal wound. Johnny Blevins had also fired, missing the sheriff but hitting Cooper's horse. Now Owens, his Winchester still at his hip, swung round and shot Johnny in the shoulder.

Mrs Blevins led the dying Cooper inside, while Owens retreated to the street to cover both sides of the Blevins' house, firing at Cooper when he spotted him through the window.

It was now Mose Roberts' turn for some action. He leapt through a door or a window in a corner of the house, pistol in hand. Once again Owens proved master of the situation, for he threw himself to one side of a wagon and mortally wounded Mose before he could fire his six-shooter. His life ebbing swiftly away, Mose Roberts staggered back into the house, whose inmates were now in a state of sheer horror, all but one.

This was Sam Houston Blevins, who had not taken to crime yet himself, but burned to avenge his kinsfolk. He could not get Johnny Blevins to give up his gun, so seized the dying Andy Cooper's, then rushed straight out of the front door, his desperate mother trying to hold him back without success. But before the brave youth could open up on Owens, the sheriff's Winchester caused him to fall back dead into his stricken mother's arms.

A silence fell on the street, broken only by the weeping of women and the groans of Johnny Blevins. Owens stared hard at the house for some moments, then turned his back on it and walked away, leaving a nightmare behind him. After a fight that had not lasted more than a minute the only man left alive in that house of death was Johnny Blevins.

Owens was thirty-five when he fought that classic, epic battle. Naturally, it did his career no harm, and, later, his wife managed to get him to shorten his hair and sober up his style of dress. He became a prosperous businessman, dying in 1919 – with his boots off.

above
The Oriental Saloon in Tombstone.

below
Copies of this photograph of three victims of the Gunfight at the OK Corral were captioned: 'Murder on the Streets of Tombstone'. From left to right are Tom and Frank McLaury and Billy Clanton.

Chapter 6
Light and Lively Ladies

Soiled Doves

From the beginning there were the respectable women and the 'soiled doves', and everything was done to see that they met as little as possible. The Californian gold rush set the pattern. Typical was the episode of Big Annie, the gal who ran a back-street fandango parlour in Columbia. One day Annie staggered out of a bar and lurched into the local schoolmistress, forcing the good lady into the road. The teacher had to raise her skirt ever so delicately in order to shake the dust off it, upon which drunken Annie rightly observed that the schoolmistress walked on two legs, like Annie and other females.

This kind of talk was too much for the town, which by any standards was no Sunday School. The volunteer fire department went to work that very night and pumped a flood of water into the fandango parlour, causing Big Annie's clients to exit hastily and Annie herself to leave town for good.

There was such a shortage of women in the mining camps of California that men came many miles just to look at one. Loneliness was rampant and no spinster, however ill-favoured, need despair. And

opposite
Timberline, a Dodge City 'soiled dove'.

top
Whooping it up in an Abilene dance hall.

left
'Squirrel-tooth' Alice of Dodge City. Note the live squirrel.

above
Billy, one of the gals of Chicago Joe's in Helena, Montana.

right through the period of this book there was still a shortage of women in the West outside the big cities. Respectable women are only incidentally the concern of this chapter, though it must be stressed that many of them rank as supreme heroes of the West, those that endured the hard, long, often dangerous crossings to Oregon, California and elsewhere, and those – often the same women – who endured backbreaking hardships, primitive conditions, and terrible loneliness in isolated homesteads on the endless plains.

The soiled doves were certainly not lonely, and many were as hard as granite. Considering the life they led and where they led it, they needed to be, though few can have been as callous as the girl in Dodge City who, after a man had had his brains blown out at the bar, rushed over and rubbed her hands on the floor in his blood. She then yelled: 'Cock-a-doodle-doo!' and clapped her hands, sending spots of blood over her dress and the clothes of those around her. A buffalo hunter watching the grisly scene was so shaken by the 'wicked bitch' that he returned to his camp to drink on his own rather than in such monstrous company.

Big cities had splendid 'bagnios', as the brothels/bawdy houses were sometimes called in print, but the men who feature in this book were rarely to be found in such elegant surroundings. The 'girls' they met in cowtowns, mining camps, or end-of-track shanty towns tended to live in 'cribs' – small, sparsely

Mattie Silks (left), in her old age. A high-class Colorado madam, she is seen here with a favourite racehorse.

*The author owes the bawdy epitaph on page 125 to Don Ashbaugh's *Nevada's Turbulent Yesterdays*.

left
Suffolk-born Poker Alice Tubbs in her youthful prime.

below
Poker Alice in old age.

furnished rooms close by, or attached to, the dance halls and saloons where they worked. Girls descended in their hundreds from many parts of the nation to where the action was, and some, as Joseph W. Snell relates in his *Painted Ladies of the Cowtowns*, were listed in directories under euphemisms: 'horizontally employed', 'night worker' etc., while the occupation of Ettie Baldwin in the 1870 census in Ellsworth was written in red ink as 'squirms in the dark'. Fines from the girls and bawdy house keepers were a splendid source of revenue for a town, while newspapers vied with each other in reporting details of the more public exploits of the soiled doves, especially popular events being when they fought men or one another. In one Dodge City fight onlookers could note that 'Tufts of hair, calico, snuff and gravel flew like fur in a cat fight, and before we could distinguish how the battle waned a chunk of dislocated leg grazed our ear and a cheer from the small boys announced that a battle was lost and won.'

The girls made as much money as possible as fast as they could, and disease and an early death, sometimes suicide, was the fate of many of them. The biggest killer was tuberculosis. Just a few managed to make good marriages, some others to leave the business. Some, like Dora Hand, who was murdered by mistake because she was in a bed where her killer expected to find someone else, when he fired four shots through a wall, were genuinely and widely popular. Dora was given one of the finest funerals Dodge City had witnessed, while a whore in Pioche, Nevada, must have been quite a gal to inspire this inscription on her tombstone:

Here lies the body of Virginia Marlotte,
She was born a virgin and died a harlot.
For eighteen years she preserved her virginity –
*That's a damned good record for this vicinity.**

Then there were the lady criminals and the 'characters', and those who were both.

Poker Alice

Pride of place among the characters, and British-born to boot, must go to the lady gambler, 'Poker Alice' Tubbs (1851–1930), who spent the

left
Pauline Cushman, a Civil War Union spy, whose career declined and fell in the West.

below
A dance hall in Cripple Creek, Colorado, in the 1890s.

first twelve years of her life in Suffolk as the daughter of a Sudbury schoolmaster. The family moved to America, and when Alice was nineteen she married an engineer, Frank Duffield, in Colorado. Frank was killed in a mining accident the next year and Alice, instead of turning to teaching, took up poker and was soon dealing cards in a saloon on a percentage basis. 'Poker Alice' was born, and highly successful Alice was. She was soon packing a pistol and smoking big cigars, and was to be seen in many a wild boom town, her appearance (the cigar apart) and accent fooling many mere males into thinking they were about to make easy money. She was working for Bob Ford, slayer of Jesse James, when he was shot in Creede, Colorado, then moved to Deadwood, where she worked in a saloon alongside another gambler, William Tubbs. One day Tubbs was accused of cheating by a drunken miner, who went for him with a Bowie knife. But before the blade found its target, a shot in the arm made him drop the knife. 'Poker Alice' had winged him with her six-shooter. The pair of gamblers were soon united in marriage. But alas, soon after they had settled down to adopt seven orphans and raise chickens, the lady gambler, who

left
When there were no women available in the West for dancing, men took their parts – as shown here at a miners' ball in Cripple Creek, Colorado.

right
A saloon girl, as portrayed in the *National Police Gazette* in 1886.

below and opposite, below
Martine Carol as Lola Montez in Max Ophüls's film *Lola Montès* (1955). Lola Montez was born in Ireland, became the mistress of Ludwig I of Bavaria, then astounded Californian miners by her presence, if not by the dance in which she fought off spiders. Her lack of talent was next offered to Australian miners.

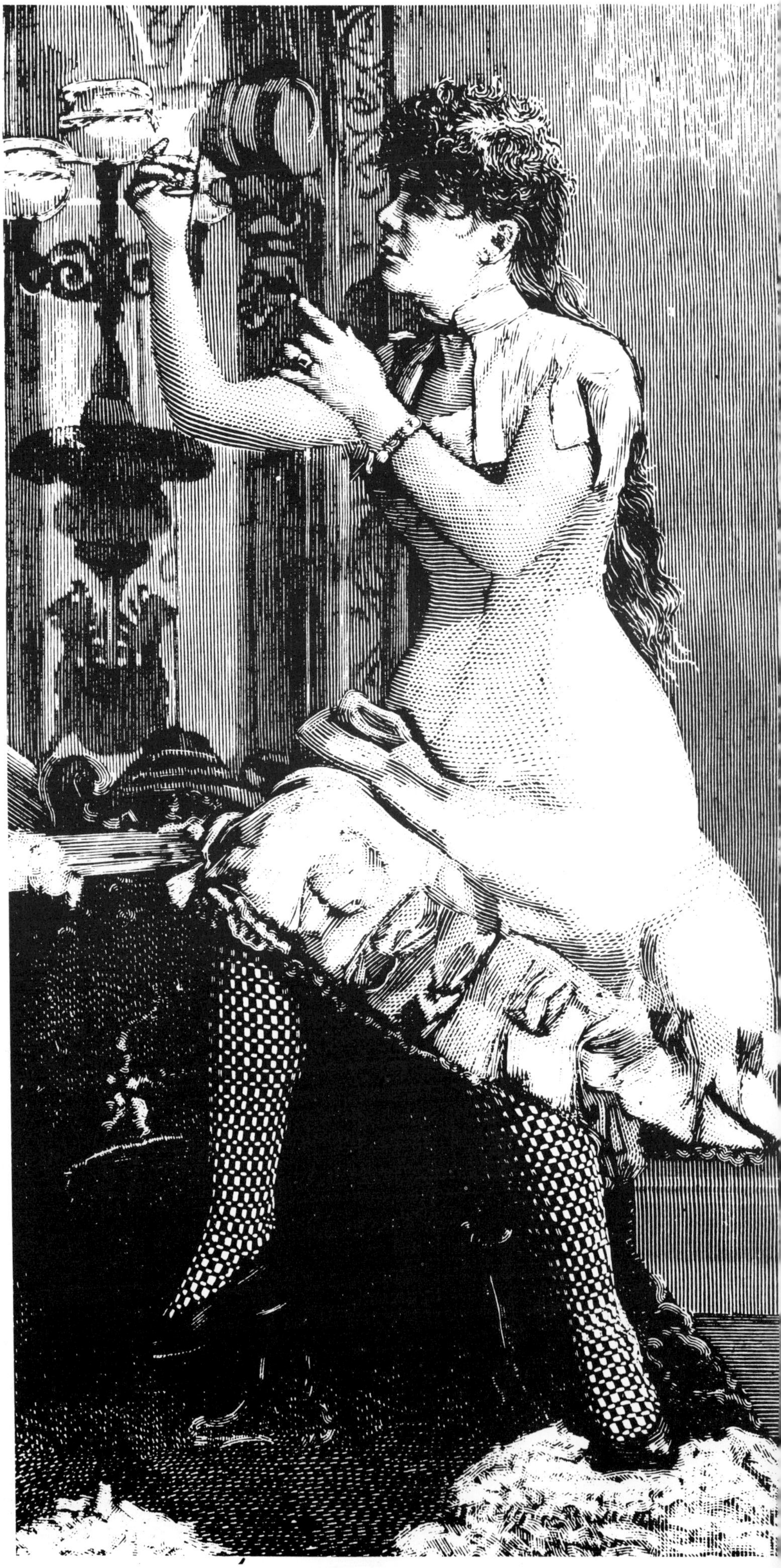

above
The gentleman performer seems to be keeping a wary eye on the opposition in this wild and woolly Western scene.

once said: 'I have never run a crooked game and never gamble on a Sunday', lost another husband. Tubbs died of pneumonia. Having pawned her engagement ring to get a grave dug, she won the money back in a saloon after the funeral.

She tried sheep farming and even married again, but separated, then returned to what she was best at, the gaming tables. She opened a club near Fort Meade, South Dakota, in 1912, and the soldiers made her prosperous all over again. But one night some drunken troopers tried to get in after hours. Fearing they might be out to rob her, she fired a shot through the door and one of the men fell dead. She was found guilty at her trial, but the judge let her go, saying: 'I cannot find it in my heart to send a white-haired lady to the penitentiary.'

That was the end of soldiers coming to her club, for the authorities put it out of bounds. Finally, she retired to a ranch and, when she was seventy-nine, was told by a doctor that she was too old for an operation. He made the mistake of saying that it would be a gamble even if she was young and strong.

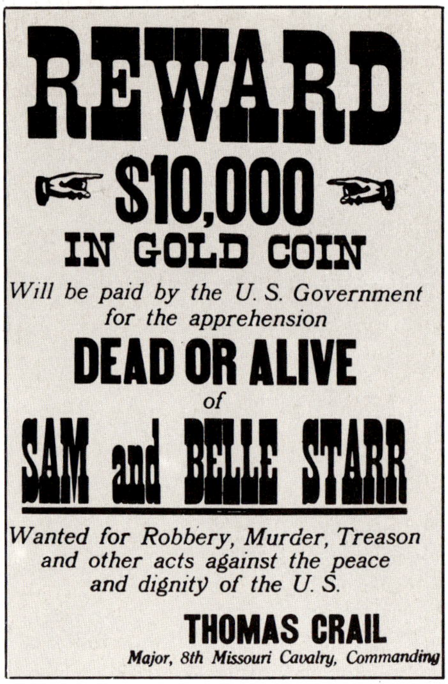
REWARD

$10,000

IN GOLD COIN

Will be paid by the U. S. Government for the apprehension

DEAD OR ALIVE

of

SAM and BELLE STARR

Wanted for Robbery, Murder, Treason and other acts against the peace and dignity of the U. S.

THOMAS CRAIL

Major, 8th Missouri Cavalry, Commanding

above
Sam Starr was a Cherokee, who, like Belle, died a violent death.

below
Belle Starr's cabin at Younger's Bend, Oklahoma. She was a lady who liked outlaws.

opposite
Belle Starr, with one of her 'husbands', Blue Duck.

Alice rose to the bait and told him to go ahead. She lost.

Belle Starr

Even more flamboyant and much less reputable was Belle Starr, who today would be dubbed a crime groupie, for she adored badmen. A James fan, she bore their ally Cole Younger a daughter, bore her first husband, rustler Jim Reed, a son, then, when he was killed, headed for Indian Territory where she married Sam Starr, a Cherokee outlaw. She must have been reasonably good-looking in her early days, whatever later photographs suggest, for now, when acting as organisation woman for local criminals, she was apparently able to seduce deputies if bribery failed to let their captives go free. Of course, it may have been the shortage of women.

She was a thorn in Judge Parker's flesh, for there was never enough evidence against her when she was brought in. But finally she was jailed for stealing a neighbour's horses, serving nine months. Her speech to one reporter suggests she would have been equally at home as a lady pirate two centuries earlier –

left
Calamity Jane enjoying a drink of beer. She used to spin yarns about herself and Wild Bill Hickok, but it seems that they were not even 'just good friends'.

below
At least Calamity lies near her alleged sweetheart, Wild Bill, in death, the place being a beautiful cemetery above Deadwood, South Dakota.

opposite
Calamity Jane, liar, plainswoman and Frontier character. She seems to have been a good-natured gal.

'I am a friend to any brave and gallant outlaw. There are three or four jolly good fellows on the dodge now in my section, and when they come to my house they are welcome, for they are my friends.'

After her handsome Cherokee was shot, she took up with a bandit named Blue Duck, who was soon under sentence of death. Good lawyers hired by the adoring Belle got him life instead, and she even got her son by Reed off scot-free when he should have served a seven-year stretch.

Finally, Belle's luck ran out. In 1889 she was murdered, probably by her latest husband Jim July, a Creek. He had, so the story goes, tried to have her killed for $200 and when his choice of assassin refused the assignment, he uttered the following memorable words – 'Hell – I'll kill the old hag myself and spend the money for whiskey.' Hollywood's Belle Starrs have included such un-haggish lovelies as Jane Russell and Gene Tierney.

Calamity Jane

As for Hollywood's Calamity Janes, Jane Russell, Yvonne de Carlo, Doris Day and Jean Arthur have

88522

been among them. There are some portraits of her which suggest she was by no means totally ill favoured, and she was a likeable girl. The trouble was, even by Frontier standards, she was a monumental liar, to such an extent that it is virtually impossible to write even a short accurate history of her. She claimed at various times to be or have been an Indian-fighter, a Pony Express rider, a scout, a bullwhacker, a gunfighter, a miner, etc. It is sounder to say that she was a whore, a camp follower, and, finally, an alcoholic. The historian who suggested that her liking for male clothing indicated that she probably suffered from a kind of 'pseudo-hermaphroditism' (Clarence Paine in 'Calamity Jane – Man, Woman or Both?', an article in the Chicago Westerners' Brand Book, September, 1945) may be right, but the fact remains that the feminine side could be strong. Her record as a nurse in Deadwood during a smallpox epidemic was a fine one.

She was born anywhere between 1844 and 1852 in Princeton, Missouri, perhaps, and it is reasonably safe to call her Martha Jane Cannary. In the late 1860s she seems to have been providing troops' comforts, then joining the Union Pacific workforce in Wyoming. She may have actually worked by day as well as by night and was remembered as a 'good-hearted hussy, hard as nails'. As long as the men gave her their old clothes, she did not mind making nothing out of them.

In her imaginative autobiography she made much of her time as a scout – which she may never have been – and she gave one of a number of explanations as to how she got her nickname, how she brought back a wounded officer who hailed her as 'Calamity Jane, heroine of

below
Eleanor Dumont – Minnie the Gambler – orders the cards counted, suspecting one George Devol of cheating. She was right: there were sixty-two cards.

opposite, left
Rose of the Cimarron, a myth-ridden gal who lived in Oklahoma in the wild days of Bill Doolin.

opposite, right
'Cattle Annie' and 'Little Britches', juvenile delinquents in the Doolin era, otherwise known as 'Oklahoma's girl bandits'. They finished up in prison.

But if she did mourn tearfully and alcoholically, she was soon in fine form again, for, we are told, she caused such an uproar in a brothel some days later that the madam locked her in a closet. Calamity's language was apparently far too strong for the local soiled doves.

Joseph Rosa has summed the next twenty-seven years of her life up, writing: 'She bummed her way around the Frontier.' The story steadily saddens. In 1901, a Mrs Josephine Blake found her dirty, drunk and ill in a bawdy house in – unbelievably – Horr, Montana, and persuaded her to take part in the Pan-American Exposition at Buffalo, New York. All she was asked to do was sit in a small hut and sell copies of her life story. After a number of disturbances, liquid and otherwise, she returned to the West, where the disturbances continued. At Billings, she lined up some naked prostitutes and had them dancing to the accompaniment of earthy comments and pistol shots.

In 1903, she became seriously ill in Terry, South Dakota, and some

the Plains'. He didn't. What is certain is that in later life she would enter a saloon, announce 'I'm Calamity Jane and this drink's on the house!' and regularly get it.

Several hopeful authorities relate how she was smuggled into the Custer expedition to the Black Hills (or was in Crook's against the Sioux?) and how one evening, when some of the soldiers were bathing in the nude, they saw Calamity and suggested she joined them. Which she did, until an officer who happened to be passing by noticed that one of the soldiers looked a little different.

Her time in Deadwood in 1876 has given rise to rumours, eagerly promoted by her, that she was Wild Bill Hickok's lover, that she was his wife, that she divorced him so that he could marry Agnes Lake. Despite claims, counterclaims and every sort of optimistic supposition, also faked evidence, there seems little doubt that she had at least met him.

right
Annie Oakley was nicknamed 'Little Sure Shot' by the Sioux chief Sitting Bull, so impressed was he by her shooting. So were others, as the medals indicate.

below
Annie Oakley was pretty and petite, which, combined with her exceptional marksmanship, made her a unique attraction in Buffalo Bill's Wild West Show. One of her show-stoppers involved leaping over a table after two clay pigeons had been released, picking up her rifle, and bringing them both down.

friends hastened from Deadwood to see her. She became delirious and babbled of a daughter in North Dakota. (The reader has been spared Calamity's alleged matrimonial arrangements. As Andrew Blewett wrote in an excellent article in the English Westerners' Brand Book of January 1963, about her, 'Calamity's list of husbands is so formidable that it makes the most promiscuous Hollywood actress seem a model of rectitude.' How many were genuine husbands is sheer conjecture.)

She died on 1 August 1903, and friends claimed that her last wish had been 'Bury me next to Bill'. This was done, and the same friends changed her death date to August 2, the twenty-seventh anniversary of Hickok's death. The pair, as was noted earlier, are linked in death as they never were in life.

Her funeral was a grand affair, though, like everything else about her, the number of mourners is disputed, from a few hundred to ten thousand. And she remains to this day the most famous of all Western women. Annie Oakley? 'Little Sure Shot', even after *Annie Get Your Gun*, has never been so famous, besides which she was an Easterner, who only visited the West on tour. And whatever anyone says about Calamity, she was all Westerner.

Chapter 7

End of an Era

It is easier to put a date to the end of the Frontier than to the ending of the old West, wild or otherwise. Officially, the Frontier came to an end in the mid-'90s when the last free land, the 160 acres offered to everyone by the Homestead Act, was used up. Or one could claim that the Frontier finally ended with the last land rush into Oklahoma in 1911.

The turn of the century saw most of the West tamed, yet, as we have seen, the Arizona Rangers under Captain Burton Mossman and others were functioning superbly between 1901 and 1909, functioning because they were still needed to curb the lawlessness that still lingered in the remoter areas of the territory. Yet the day of the gunfighter had really ended by 1900. The telegraph and telephone, the general spread of law and order, made it harder for bands of outlaws to disappear into the wilds. When Butch Cassidy and the Sundance Kid set out for South America in 1902 it was a sure sign that the old days were finally over. They and the Wild Bunch and other badmen had been able to operate from remote lairs in Utah and Wyoming; their careers reached a climax with a

A famous picture of part of the Wild Bunch. From left to right: (standing) Bill Carver and Harvey Logan, alias Kid Curry; (sitting) Harry Longbaugh (the Sundance Kid), Ben 'The Tall Texan' Kilpatrick, and Robert 'George' Leroy Parker, alias Butch Cassidy.

opposite, above
The exterior of an express car blown up by Butch Cassidy's gang at Wilcox, Wyoming, in June, 1899.

opposite, below
The interior of a car blown up by the Wild Bunch at Tipton, Wyoming, in August, 1900.

left
The Sundance Kid and Etta Place, photographed in New York en route for South America.

below
Hole-in-the-Wall was a dream hideout for badmen in a remote area of Wyoming.

bottom
The hand-picked posse boarding their special train to hunt down the Wild Bunch.

right
The Apache Kid was treated so badly by whites that he switched from loyal scout to ruthless renegade. He was never captured.

below
Tom Ketchum was wrongly called 'Black Jack' Ketchum because of a confusion with 'Black Jack' Christian.

bottom
'Black Jack' Christian, an outlaw in the Southwest until his death in 1897.

sensational series of train robberies at the turn of the century. But Pinkerton men were after them and then the Union Pacific brought its famous special train, complete with a very determined posse of gunfighters, into action. It was common sense to clear out.

Until recently it seemed that Butch – real name, Robert Leroy Parker – and the Sundance Kid, actually Harry Longbaugh, perished in Bolivia, but it now seems virtually certain that other Americans died in the gun battle with the police. Butch's sister has proved to almost everyone's satisfaction that the pair returned quietly to the States – and lived quietly for many years. Butch was a most unusual outlaw leader in that he was genuinely likeable and claimed with apparent honesty that he had never ever killed a man.

Perhaps the true ending of the Wild West came in 1912 when Ben Kilpatrick, alias the Tall Texan, staged the last hold-up of a train in the traditional way, his assistant being Nick Grider. Ben had been a star member of the old Wild Bunch, but he was no longer the man he had been in the old dynamite days.

The place chosen was Dryden, Texas, the railroad selected for this historic hold-up being the Southern Pacific. The westbound express had just pulled out of town when Ben Kilpatrick climbed into the locomotive cab and at first everything seemed to be going well in the traditional manner. The train was halted, the mail and express cars were detached from the passenger coaches and run a mile up track.

right
John Sontag caused Wells Fargo a lot of trouble until he was mortally wounded near Visilia, California, in 1904. He is seen dead or dying in a haystack.

above
After a notable career as an outlaw leader, Tom Ketchum achieved even more notoriety in death when his head was torn away from his body at his hanging in April, 1901.

right
Ned Christie, a notorious Cherokee Indian outlaw who defended himself in a log-fort in Indian Territory before he was blasted out with dynamite and shot down as he tried to escape.

below
Gradually, vicious hostility towards sheep and sheepmen died down, but they were still in danger in parts of the West less than seventy years ago.

Nick Grider kept the crew under surveillance as the Tall Texan took a look at the two cars. His reflexes were not what they were, however, for he allowed himself to be distracted by David Trousdale, the express messenger, who battered the big man's brains out with an ice mallet. Then Trousdale picked up Ben's rifle and waited.

When he had waited long enough, he fired two shots, which brought Nick Grider to the scene, and as he began to clamber into the car, he was shot through the head. Only a few weeks earlier, Ben Kilpatrick had told a newspaper editor that – after a nine-and-a-half-year stretch in prison – he was a reformed character. He claimed he was going to get a flock of sheep and convince the world that he could be a good citizen instead of an outlaw. As the editor noted on hearing news of his subject's lapse from grace, 'Alas, for good intentions!'

opposite, above right
The aftermath of the last train hold-up in the old tradition – Ben Kilpatrick and Nick Grider in death.

opposite, below
Walker & McCoy's sign shop at Guthrie, Oklahoma, in 1889. The townsmen were taking over.

above
Things were quietening down when some cowboys started switching to rodeos, like this early star performer.

right
Harvey Logan, alias Kid Curry, lies dead. The date: 1903.

right
In the end the settlers won the West. This family is in front of a Wisconsin log cabin.

below
There was a final Wild West in the far North, though Dawson City on Canadian territory, near the fabulous Klondike goldfields, was kept in order so well by the Mounties that at the height of the Stampede in 1898 there was not a single killing.

Appendix One

Some Notes on Western Films

Nearly every Wild West buff, even the most scholarly, will admit that Western films were responsible for a life-long passion. Most buffs still enjoy Westerns, but that enjoyment is tempered with many reservations and much strong criticism. Some films, which are admittedly sheer visual poetry and undoubted works of art, irritate by their blatant inaccuracy. John Ford's *My Darling Clementine*, about Wyatt Earp and Tombstone, plays fast and loose with facts even if one can accept the grossly over-sympathetic portrait of Earp himself. Ford claimed he got the facts from Earp, who, being a con man, no doubt came across very well when interviewed, but he can hardly have come out with such a travesty, even if painting a rosy picture of his own prowess. Besides, Earp, like him or not, was a hard case, not a gentle creature like Mr Earp-Fonda. Needless to say, a warm romantic glow suffuses the film, which has precious little to do with turbulent Tombstone. But the film remains a masterpiece, a Frontier myth.

Westerners find it hard to accept gross distortions of fact, even when the atmosphere is right, and tend to be happier when no pretence of fact is made: Howard Hawks' *Rio Bravo* and *El Dorado*, for instance, both starring John Wayne. But when a director (Arthur Penn) presents us with the Billy the Kid story in *The Left-Handed Gun,* the historically minded buff is likely to be upset, say, at the cavalier way the young and English John Tunstall was turned into an elderly and Scottish character, simply, it may be assumed, to make him a conventional father figure. That Billy was not left-handed, but has been assumed to be so because of a famous reversed photograph, is a more forgiveable error.

The film, as opposed to Western, buff may well claim such criticisms are trivial and surely the psychological Billy of the film is full of interest?

Broncho Billy Anderson, one of the first Western stars.

right
William S. Hart, an ex-Shakespearean actor, became world famous from 1918. Unlike many that followed him, he believed in reasonable accuracy.

below
John Wayne (left) in an early starring role: *'Neath the Arizona Skies* (1934).

It is safer for the film buff to say simply that the film should solely be judged – as a film.

Westerns were born with the ten-minute one-reeler *The Great Train Robbery* (1903). The best of the early stars in Westerns was William S. Hart, not least because he was devoted to accuracy in sets and costumes, compared with those silent stars who came later. In the 1920s Tom Mix softened the image and took things more lightheartedly, and inspired a whole host of successors, perhaps the finest of them being the now little remembered Buck Jones. The 'singing cowboys' of the 1930s–50s need not detain us here, though the popularity of Gene Autry and Roy Rogers was immense. More happily, the '30s saw the first great Western, John Ford's *Stagecoach,* which made John Wayne a star. Given that even the finest Westerns have presented a romantic rather than an epic or savage West until the 1960s, when the genre, in fact, started to decline in quality, it was a wonderful period. Stars with the 'right' feel for the West included Wayne himself, Randolph Scott, James Stewart, Gary Cooper, and Joel McCrea. The younger generation are now seeing the magnificent Westerns of this period on the TV screen, which lessens some of their impact and distorts if the original was in Cinemascope, but which at least introduces them to the Westerns at their finest.

There follows a short list of Westerns which are not necessarily the finest artistically but are recommended for seekers after approximate truth. They concern the subject of this book, which means that John Ford's cavalry masterpiece, *She Wore a Yellow Ribbon*, is not included and nor are the handful of films which adequately portray the American Indian.

Stagecoach (1939). John Ford based his film on an Ernest Haycox short story. The photography, characterisation, dramatic tension and legitimate sentiment are all superb. Most buffs know by now that in the incomparable chase sequence in the desert the Apaches would have shot the horses, but where would the heart of the film have been then? The final scenes in town and the gun battle there may seem a trifle unsophisticated now, like other parts of the film, but the film remains a totally satisfying masterpiece.

Red River (1948). Directed by Howard Hawks, this is the finest

left
Henry Fonda shows Anthony Perkins a thing or two in *The Tin Star* (1957).

below, left
James Stewart in *The Man from Laramie* (1955).

below
Gary Cooper as Wild Bill Hickok in *The Plainsman* (1936), with James Ellison (right) as Buffalo Bill.

cowboy film of them all, though others, like Tom Greis's *Will Penny* (1967), are more realistic. The central role inspired John Wayne to give one of his best performances, and Montgomery Clift and John Ireland were among others who did fine work. So, of course, did Walter Brennan, the most convincing 'old-timer' of them all.

The Gunfighter (1950). Henry King directed this exceptional portrait of an ageing pistoleer, Ringo, excellently acted by Gregory Peck. Detail and atmosphere are notably good and the plot is a telling one. Ringo's reputation is his curse and, though he tries to steer clear of trouble, he is finally shot in the back by a youngster who wants the fame of the man who killed Ringo. There is an ironic ending, Ringo's friends letting the killer survive so that his reputation as a fast gun will be the death of him.

High Noon (1952). Gary Cooper starred as marshal Will Kane, and Fred Zinnemann directed this classic, mentioned in Chapter Three, about the lone lawman, just married and about to retire, who stays on in town to face killers from his past who are out to get him. As readers will have noted, lawmen could rely on help, not only from their deputies, but also from determined citizens in the old West, but given that a real life Will Kane could have expected and got help, this film is a cinematic masterpiece, its tension is masterly, and Cooper excelled himself. The screenplay was by Carl Foreman, who, as a McCarthy victim himself, created (though from a magazine story) a

right
Stagecoach (1939), the first great Western. Director: John Ford. From left to right are George Bancroft, John Wayne and Claire Trevor.

below
John Wayne in *The Shootist* (1976), an unusual and magnificent Western with a classic performance by Big John.

right
Gary Cooper in *High Noon* (1952).

left
Alan Ladd in *Shane* (1953).

below
Up go the dollar bills in the explosion in *Butch Cassidy and the Sundance Kid* (1969).

man standing alone like many had done in the McCarthy trials era. But it is a film about a marshal, not a political tract, even though John Wayne was horrified when Cooper threw his sacred badge in the dust at the film's ending. The film takes eighty-four minutes, which is approximately how long the action lasts, a fact that increases the intensity. As for the famous theme music, sung by Tex Ritter, it created an unfortunate trend, though itself a triumph.

Shane (1953). A masterpiece based on a masterpiece, the novel by Jack Schaefer. The director was George Stevens and his cast was headed by Alan Ladd (who didn't quite let the side down), Van Heflin, monumental as a pioneer, lovely Jean Arthur, Brandon de Wilde, and Jack Palance as the ultimate gunfighter in black. The scene is Wyoming and the story was partly inspired by the Johnson County War, though it is on a smaller scale. Given that there is a warm romantic glow over the film, partly because of the overpowering beauty of the photography and the location (the Grand Tetons and the valley below them), the film remains a most truthful one. Those extraordinary critics who deny that *Shane* and *High Noon* are real Westerns only show their ignorance.

To end with, four films must be mentioned, three of which are not 'straight' Westerns, but which all accurately reflect aspects of the old West. *Butch Cassidy and the Sundance Kid* (1969), though full of humour and sheer gimmickry by its director, George Roy Hill, gave a by no means inaccurate portrait of the pair of outlaws and their later career. *Paint Your Wagon* (1969), though a (first-rate) musical, had the authentic Californian gold rush feeling in several splendid sequences. (Director: Joshua Logan.) And *True Grit* (Director: Henry Hathaway), though based on a loving spoof of a dime novel (see below), gave a fair representation of Indian Territory and Judge Parker's Fort Smith, and, of course, gave John Wayne a whale of a part into the bargain. So did *The Shootist*, a magnificent 'end of an era' picture (Director: Don Siegel).

Appendix Two

Some Notes on Western Fiction

Again, these are confined to books relevant to the West of the gunfighter, which cuts down the number considerably. Some of the best novels set in the West are about the Indian Wars, e.g. Elliott Arnold's *Blood Brother*. This is not to disparage the best of the flood of Western fiction that has poured forth for a century or more, but there really is a limit to how much the average Western writer can permutate the stock Western plots. Most seekers after truth about the Wild West tend to concentrate entirely on non-fiction, gradually learning which authors supply fiction disguised as fact and which write the genuine thing.

Here is a short list of books that can be strongly recommended:
The Virginian by Owen Wister, the first major fictional work on the trans-Mississippi West. It appeared in 1902.
Riders of the Purple Sage by Zane Grey, the most notable writer of Western fiction. Like 'Doc' Holliday, he began his professional life as a dentist.
Shane by Jack Schaefer (see film section), all of whose stories on Western themes combine fine writing with a knowledge of the West.
The Hanging Tree by Dorothy Johnson, whose other stories, like Schaefer's, are all worth reading.

above, left
Clint Eastwood, king of the Spaghetti Westerns.

left
Burt Lancaster in *Lawman* (1971).

Bugles in the Afternoon by Ernest Haycox, who, thought not in the same league as Johnson or Schaefer, was a fine Western writer.
The Ox-Bow Incident by Walter von Tilburg Clark, a classic novel about lynching and its implications, which was made into a notable film.
True Grit by Charles Portis. As mentioned in the film section, a loving, brilliant spoof of a dime novel, set in Judge Parker's Fort Smith and in Indian Territory.

above
A harder look than usual at the Gunfight at the OK Corral in *Hour of the Gun* (1967), with James Garner as Wyatt Earp.

left
Ride the High Country (1962) starred two old-timers – in life and the movies: Joel McCrea and Randolph Scott in a changing West.

below
Henry Fonda looks down at Anthony Quinn in *Warlock* (1959).

Appendix Three

Suggested Reading

The bibliography of Western Americana is vast, but here is a short list of books, most of which can be obtained at large or specialist bookshops, or be ordered from them. These could form the nucleus of a serious Western library:

The American West by John A. Hawgood (London, 1967) is a good general introduction to the West as a whole, while *Frontier Justice* by Wayne Gard (Norman, Oklahoma, 1949) is a classic on the violent West, though a little out of date now. Time-Life's *The Gunfighters* (1974) is visually superb and has a good text by Paul Trachtman, but its captions sometimes badly let it down. *Great Gunfighters of the Kansas Cowtowns* by Nyle Miller and Joseph Snell (Lincoln, Nebraska, 1963) is essential reading, as is Joseph G. Rosa's *They Called Him Wild Bill* (Norman, Oklahoma, 1974). Colonel Maurice Fulton's *Lincoln County War* (University of Arizona, 1968) is the classic on the subject, and another classic is *The Texas Rangers* by Walter Prescott Webb (Austin, 1965). Naturally, all the books mentioned in the text are recommended, with one rather obvious exception.

The Wild Bunch (1968), a very violent, allegedly anti-violence Western.

Index

Numbers in italics refer to illustrations.
Films have the director's name in brackets.

Acknowledgments

The author would like to thank the following for their help and advice: Joseph W Snell and Nancy Sherbert of the Kansas State Historical Society; Elaine Gilleran and the rest of the staff of the Wells Fargo Bank History Room; Katherine Halverson of the Wyoming State Historical Society; and four fellow members of the English Westerners' Society, Jeff Burton, Colin Rickards, Joseph G Rosa and Tom Wanless. He would also like to thank Fredie Steve Harris of Houston, Texas, for tracking down pictures of the Texas Rangers.

Photographs

Arizona Historical Society, Tucson front jacket (centre right), back jacket (top and bottom insets), back flap, 63 bottom, 77, 79 top, 80 left, 80 right, 103, 115 top, 115 bottom left, 115 bottom right, 116 left, 117, 118, 119 top, 120-121, 140 top right; Culver Pictures, New York 6–7; Denver Public Library, Western History Department, Denver, Colorado endpapers, 26 top, 50, 73, 76 left, 96, 104 top, 107, 110, 119 bottom, 124, 126–127; Mary Evans Picture Library, London 128 right, 129 top; Pat Hall 92; Hamlyn Group Picture Library 144 bottom, 149 right, 152; John Judkin Memorial, Freshford Manor, Bath 24 top; Kansas State Historical Society, Topeka front jacket (bottom right), 10, 11 top, 11 bottom, 16, 17 top, 17 bottom, 21 bottom, 22 top, 34, 35, 37, 39, 40, 44 left, 44 right, 47 bottom, 48, 49 top, 49 bottom, 51 top, 51 bottom, 51 left, 52 right, 53, 54 top, 54–55, 55 top, 56 top, 56 bottom, 58 top, 58 bottom, 114, 122, 123 top, 123 bottom left; Larousse, Paris 146 top; Mansell Collection, London 129 bottom; Robin May front jacket (bottom left), 12 top left, 13, 21 top, 25, 41 top, 41 bottom, 42, 43 top, 43 bottom, 45, 46 top, 46 bottom, 47 top, 60 top, 60 bottom, 64 left, 64–65, 67, 68 top, 71, 74 bottom, 81, 82, 84 left, 85, 88 bottom, 93 left, 102 top right, 105 right, 108 right, 109, 112 top, 113, 121 bottom, 125 left, 130 top, 132 top, 132 bottom, 134, 135 right, 142 top right, 148 top, 151 bottom; Minnesota Historical Society, St Pail 28 top, 28-29, 31 right; Montana Historical Society, Helena front jacket (centre picture), 15 bottom, 123 bottom right; Museum of New Mexico, Santa Fe back jacket (main picture), 15 top, 84 right, 111, 112 bottom; National Archives, Washington D.C. 23 bottom; National Archives – *Fish and Wildlife* 74 top; National Archives – Secretary of the Interior 23 top; National Archives – US Signal Corps 19 right, 20 bottom, 22 bottom, 23 bottom, 69, 75, 87, 133, 140 top left, 141 left, 141 top; National Archives – US Signal Corps (Brady Collection) 70; National Archives – US War Department General Staff 14; National Film Archive, London 128 left, 145, 146 bottom, 147 bottom left, 148 left, 148 bottom, 151 centre; Oklahoma Historical Society, Oklahoma 130 bottom, 131; Paramount Pictures 147 top; Pinkerton's, New York 30, 137, 139 top left, 143 bottom right; Radio Times Hulton Picture Library, London front jacket (top left), 136 left, 136 right; Joseph G Rosa Collection front flap, 31 left, 98, 116 right, 125 right; Saint Joseph Museum, Saint Joseph, Missouri 18 top, 26, 27 top, 32; State Historical Society of Missouri, Columbia front jacket (top right), 19 top, 27 bottom; State Historical Society of Winsconsin, Madison front jacket (centre left), 144 top; Texas State Archives, Austin 59, 62, 63 top; Union Pacific Railroad Museum Collection, Omaha, Nebraska 18–19, 138 top, 138 bottom, 139 bottom; United Artists Corporation 150 top; University of Oregon, Eugene 142 top left; Utah State Historical Society, Salt Lake City 57, 140 bottom; Wells Fargo Bank, History Room, San Francisco, California 66; Western Americana Picture Library, Brentwood 12 top right, 12 bottom, 33 top, 33 bottom, 61, 76 right, 90, 102 top left, 126 left, 127 top, 147 bottom right, 149 left, 150 bottom, 151 top; Western History Collections, University of Oklahoma, Norman 36, 68 bottom, 72 left, 72 right, 83, 101 bottom, 102 bottom, 104 bottom, 105 left, 108 left, 138 left, 141 bottom, 142-143; Western History Research Center, University of Wyoming, Laramie 89, 91, 93 right, 94, 95 top, 97, 106; Winchester Gun Museum, New Haven, Connecticut 99 top, 99 bottom, 100 left, 100 centre, 100 right, 101 top; Wyoming State Archives and Historical Department, Cheyenne 78–79, 88 top, 95 bottom, 139 top right, 143 top right.

e Early 70s and 68 + 9 the early
d here Socalled, "Boot-Hill" or
ght killed in brawls + drun
e on, Wild Bill marshall in
ted. Boot Hill first some 70 or
This photo shows where in e
unexpectedly on 5 or six
d with the bullet in hea
rude stones and wooden